TRūE

TRūE

A TEEN DEVOTIONAL

Words from the Rock

MELODY CARLSON

Revell

a division of Baker Publishing Group
Grand Rapids, Michigan

Published by Revell
a division of Baker Publishing Group
P.O. Box 6287, Grand Rapids, MI 49516-6287
www.revellbooks.com

Printed in the United States of America

Library of Congress Cataloging-in-Publication Data
Carlson, Melody.
    True : a teen devotional / Melody Carlson.
      p.   cm. — (Words from the Rock ; bk. 1)
    ISBN 978-0-8007-3254-7 (pbk.)
    1. Christian teenagers—Prayers and devotions. 2. Bible. N.T. Matthew—Meditations. I. Title.
  BV4850.C335 2008
  242'.63—dc22   2008019660

Contents

Introduction

*M*aybe you've heard this before: "Jesus is the Rock." But what does it really mean? And what does it mean to you personally?

I was fifteen when I went from being a flat-out atheist to a sold-out believer. And, trust me, my life did a complete 180-degree turnaround, but I didn't have a clue as to what my next move should be. As far as the Bible went, I didn't know 1 Chronicles from 1 Corinthians, and being in church felt like being in a foreign country with a whole new language. In other words, although I was found, I was feeling pretty lost.

But one of the very first things I learned as a new believer was that Jesus was not simply my new best friend, he was my Rock as well. And I needed a rock. I needed someone I could lean on and rely on. Someone strong and steady and immovable and sturdy. Someone I could build my life on and who would never wimp out on me. *I needed a rock*—and that Rock was Jesus.

As the years passed, I got more comfortable with the Bible and the church and things like praying and worshiping. And after a lot of years, I got almost *too* comfortable. I knew a lot of the Bible by heart, I was teaching Bible studies, and I spoke nearly perfect "Christianese." Consequently, I began to take spiritual things a little for granted, and this bothered me—in fact, it bothered me a lot.

So, what did I do? I went back to the Rock. Instead of trying to become "smarter" or trying to become "theological" and understand more of the Bible, I decided to go back to Jesus (the Rock). I got myself a redlined Bible (the kind where Jesus's words are in red type), and I let myself read only the red lines—just the words from the Rock. And, man, was I blessed.

That's the whole point of this devotional—I want to share Jesus's words with you. I want to share verses that have changed and strengthened my life, and I hope they will do the same for you. The primary Scriptures used in this devotional are quotes from Jesus—words from the Rock—and believe me, they totally rock!

1

More Than Food

*It is written: "Man does not live on bread alone,
but on every word that comes from the mouth
of God."*

Matthew 4:4 NIV

I'm sure it's no coincidence that some of Jesus's first recorded words in the New Testament were about something we can all relate to—food. And although he was addressing Satan (Jesus hadn't eaten in weeks, and the devil had been tempting him to turn stones into bread), these rock-solid words were meant for everyone.

So, imagine you're starving. You're hungrier than you've ever been in your entire life. You haven't eaten in days, and all you can think about is food, food, food. Whether it's a Big Mac and fries or a pepperoni pizza or even sushi, you are so hungry you might actually sell your soul for something to eat. That's right where Satan had Jesus—or so he thought.

But what was Jesus's response to Satan's temptation? Even in his starved and emaciated state, Jesus told Satan that it took more than food to sustain life. He said that it was God's very words that would keep him alive. But what did that mean?

Jesus was our example in that he lived his life in a very tight relationship with God. In the same way that some people must stay connected (via text messaging, cell phones, email, instant messages, etc.), Jesus related to God on an ongoing, never-ending basis. It was this tight and constant connection that gave Jesus the power and strength to do all he did. He stayed tuned to God and relied on God's communication even more than he relied on food. It was his lifeline. And that's what he wants for us too—to connect and stay tuned to him, to realize we need him even more than we need food.

My Prayer

Dear God,
It's easy to know when I need food because I hear my stomach growling, and it's all I can think about. But it's not always so obvious to know how much I need you and your words. Teach me to tune in to you—to listen to you—and to understand that your words can sustain me better and longer than my favorite meal. Amen.

Stone
for the Journey

I need God's words more than I need food.

Final Word

I have hidden your word in my heart, that I might not sin against you.

Psalm 119:11 NLT

2
Make God Number One

Words from the Rock

> *Go away Satan! The Scriptures say: "Worship the Lord your God and serve only him."*
>
> Matthew 4:10 CEV

This was something else Jesus said when he was out in the desert being tempted by Satan. He'd already told the devil that it took more than food to live. And when Satan tried to get Jesus to do a cheap trick to prove he was God's Son, Jesus told that lowlife that it was wrong to use God's power just to show off. And in this verse Jesus must've been totally fed up with the devil because he simply told the loser to get lost.

Jesus also pointed out that we are to serve and worship *only God*— no one and nothing else. Seems simple, and yet how often we forget. Consider what you spend your time thinking about. Maybe it's a special someone, like your most recent crush. Or maybe it's an activity you enjoy, like a sport or shopping. The thing is, if you spend a LOT of time thinking and obsessing over this particular person or thing, it becomes a lot like worship. And you have to ask yourself, *Who am I serving?*

God wants us to put him in that *first-place position*. He wants to be the top priority in our lives. It's okay to have other loved ones beneath him, but God wants to own that number one spot. And when he does, everything else will begin to fall into place.

My Prayer

Dear God,
Thank you for showing me how important it is to keep you first and foremost in my life. Help me to remember this when other people and things try to crowd into that place. Show me how I can serve and worship you above all else! Amen.

Stone
for the Journey

I will keep God in the first-place position in my heart.

Final Word

> *The LORD is king!*
> *Let the earth rejoice!*
> *Let the farthest coastlands be glad.*
>
> Psalm 97:1 NLT

3

Time to Change

From that time Jesus began to preach, saying, "Change your hearts and lives, because the kingdom of heaven is near."

Matthew 4:17 NCV

lthough this is a short verse, it's totally power packed. After spending those long, hot, and hungry weeks in the desert, being tempted by Satan, Jesus was now starting his earthly ministry. And the first thing he told everyone listening was that it was *time for change*. He told them they needed to admit that they'd been doing things wrong, that they needed to tell God they were sorry, and that they were ready to do things differently. Jesus told the people it was time to repent!

And then he told them that the reason it was time for this kind of change was because God's kingdom was beginning—right then and there! God was going to do some amazing and wonderful things in their lives, and they needed to be ready for what was coming their way.

It's the same way with us. When we admit that we've blown it, and when we tell God we're sorry and that we really want to change, it's like we're inviting him to build his kingdom right in our hearts. It's like we're asking him to rule and reign inside us—and that's when things really begin to change. And here's the cool deal—it's not really a one-time-only thing; it's something we can and need to do on a regular basis. We need to tell God when we mess up. We need to say we're sorry. And we need to want to change. Then he comes into our lives and helps us to do that.

My Prayer

Dear God,
I admit that I blow it a lot. Help me to remember to come directly to you each time I do. And then help me to change, so you can take up residence inside me. Thank you! Amen.

Stone
for the Journey

I will turn from my mistakes and put them behind me.

Final Word

> *Get rid of these evil thoughts and ask God to forgive you.*

Acts 8:22 CEV

4

Follow Me

Words from the Rock

Come with me! I will teach you how to bring in people instead of fish.

Matthew 4:19 CEV

*W*hen Jesus gave this invitation to follow him, he was talking to some fishermen along the Sea of Galilee. They were going about their normal business, which was actually very hard labor, and Jesus paused to tell them that if they would leave their boats and nets, he would teach them to do something much better than fish for bass and perch. He would transform them into men who fished for the souls of men and women.

Now, you'd think those tough, crusty fishermen would've been shocked by that crazy-weird invitation, but they weren't. They stepped away from their boats and the life they knew like it was no big deal. They walked away from what had been their livelihood, and they simply followed Jesus. And everything Jesus promised them eventually came true.

Jesus invites you to follow him in a very similar way. He promises that he has better ways of doing things. He has a better kind of work for you to do. He has something really special and amazing in store . . . *if you will just follow him*. But sometimes that sounds crazy-weird—like how do you step away from your life and just follow him? Here's the secret—you don't have to figure it all out. You simply follow where he leads.

My Prayer

Dear God,
I want to follow you. I want to believe you have a unique plan for me, just as you did for those fishermen. But I know believing that requires a lot of trust on my part. Help me to have that kind of faith.
Amen.

Stone
for the Journey

I choose to follow God wherever he leads.

Final Word

I did this as an example so that you should do as I have done for you.

John 13:15 NCV

5
End of Your Rope

Words from the Rock

You're blessed when you're at the end of your rope. With less of you there is more of God and his rule.

Matthew 5:3 Message

*S*ometimes Jesus said things that didn't make complete sense to everyone, at least at first. Hopefully the truth soaked in later. But sometimes Jesus said things that sounded like an oxymoron—like "you're a *lucky loser*" or "isn't that a *great disaster*." Okay, those weren't Jesus's exact words, but sometimes the things he said made people scratch their heads and wonder.

When Jesus taught the Sermon on the Mount (Matthew 5–7), he spoke of a variety of ways that people were blessed. And the first one he described was how we'd be blessed when we reached the end of our rope. Huh? Was he saying we should be glad when we have nothing left to give, when we're spent, worn-out, or beaten? Seriously, who feels happy about that?

But Jesus knew something we didn't. He knew that as soon as we figured out that we'd done all we could and still failed—that was when we might begin to look to God for assistance. When we hit an impossibly tough spot, we'd cry out for help. Because, unfortunately, most of us have to be exhausted and beaten up and backed into a corner before we realize that God is just waiting for us to invite him to help.

So Jesus was saying that if we can figure out that truth sooner in our everyday lives—if we can grasp and accept that we're not strong enough, smart enough, or quick enough—*then life will get better.* When we step aside and allow God to be our strength, our wisdom, and our protection, that's when we'll be blessed!

My Prayer

Dear God,
Sometimes I forget just how weak I really am. Teach me to figure it out sooner. I try to do things on my own, and I make a total mess. Help me to remember how much I need you as I recognize how inadequate I really am. And then I can be glad you made me like this—just so you can bless me with more of you!
Amen.

Stone
for the Journey

I give God my weakness in exchange for his strength.

Final Word

He [the Lord] replied, "My kindness is all you need. My power is strongest when you are weak." So if Christ keeps giving me his power, I will gladly brag about how weak I am.

2 Corinthians 12:9 CEV

6

Good Loser

Words from the Rock

*You're blessed when you feel you've lost what is
most dear to you. Only then can you be embraced
by the One most dear to you.*

Matthew 5:4 Message

The next blessing Jesus described in his mountaintop sermon is similar to the first one—meaning it sounds a bit like an oxymoron. Remember the "lucky loser" line? Well, this particular blessing involves personal loss. Admit it, it's hard to get excited about losing someone or something you love. But Jesus said you'd be blessed when you lose whatever is most valuable to you.

And that's a little scary. I mean, think about it. What is so precious to you that you cannot imagine living on the planet without it? Is it a person—like your best friend, a family member, your latest crush? Or maybe it's a thing—a great car, your computer, your cell phone, or a pet. How would you feel if it was suddenly taken from you?

Okay, maybe that's something you'd rather not think about right now. Or maybe you've already experienced that loss in some form. Whatever the case, Jesus is saying that when you know what it's like to lose whatever you love the most, you will then understand what it means to be gathered up into God's arms and loved like you've *never been loved before.* It's not that God doesn't love you now, but this is his guarantee that if you suffer a painful loss, he has a very special way of comforting you.

If you think about it, that's an amazing promise. And if you believe it and take it seriously, that promise can give you the confidence to go bravely through life, because you'll know that no matter what happens, even if what you love most is taken, God will be there ready to love you in a way that will blow your socks off—a way that's beyond any earthly form of love. That's an awesome blessing!

My Prayer

Dear God,
Help me to understand how huge your love for me really is. Whether or not I've experienced a big loss in my life, help me to realize that you are able to make up for it in ways I cannot begin to imagine. I want my faith to grow as I choose to trust you with whatever loss has come or will come into my life. Help me to reach the place where I know I am blessed no matter what.
Amen.

Stone
for the Journey

I can trust God with my loss.

Final Word

> *If you want to save your life, you will destroy it. But if you give up your life for me, you will save it.*
>
> Luke 9:24 CEV

7

Real Contentment

Words from the Rock

You're blessed when you're content with just who you are—no more, no less. That's the moment you find yourselves proud owners of everything that can't be bought.

Matthew 5:5 Message

How many people do you know who can honestly say, "I like who I am and how I look, and I like my mind and my abilities . . . and I wouldn't change a thing about myself"? Yeah, right. It's just not that easy, is it?

Not that we don't wish we could live in that happy place and have that kind of positive attitude. But it just seems impossible—at least in a 24-7 kind of way. And maybe we even try. But get real—how many of us jump out of bed every single morning and look in the mirror and say, "Wow, awesome"?

Something about the human condition seems to have destined us for discontent and comparisons. We might not like to admit that we sometimes long for more, but most of us have been there, done that—whether it's wishing we looked like some hot celebrity or simply had straight hair and a different eye color. And, whether we wish we had as much money as Donald Trump or just enough money to buy an old used car, we know we're not always satisfied with the status quo.

Yet Jesus said we'd be blessed when we're able to see ourselves as we really are and go, "Yeah, all right . . . I'm cool with that." When we get to the place in life where we're truly content with ourselves and the way God made us, we will finally be free of the comparison game, petty jealousy, and general discontent. And, seriously, what a blessing that would be!

My Prayer

Stone
for the Journey

I choose to be happy with the way God made me.

Dear God,
I confess that I'm not always content with who I am. Okay, that might be an understatement. But I pray that you'll help me see myself the way you see me. I pray that you'll remind me that you made me like this for a reason and that I can trust you with that. I give all that I am to you, and I ask for your help in finding a place of contentment—because I can't get there without you. Thank you!
Amen.

Final Word

A devout life does bring wealth, but it's the rich simplicity of being yourself before God. Since we entered the world penniless and will leave it penniless, if we have bread on the table and shoes on our feet, that's enough.

1 Timothy 6:6–8 Message

8

Hungry for God?

> *You're blessed when you've worked up a good appetite for God. He's food and drink in the best meal you'll ever eat.*
>
> Matthew 5:6 Message

This might be one of the more obvious blessings from Jesus's Sermon on the Mount. Jesus was simply pointing out that we'll be blessed when we hunger and thirst for God as much as we do for food and drink. Simple enough . . . and yet most of us don't live our lives like that on a daily basis. Usually our stomachs growl for food a whole lot more quickly than our hearts cry out for God.

But have you ever noticed how many Bible verses compare God and Jesus to food and drink? And do you wonder why that is? Okay, maybe that's obvious too. Food and drink are things we all enjoy on a pretty regular basis. They're a part of life and things that healthy people aren't willing to give up. Think about it. It doesn't take more than, say, six hours without eating or drinking before we wonder when the next meal is coming.

Jesus was saying that if we desire God the way we long for our next hot meal, we will be really blessed. That's because we will have more and more of God in our lives—we'll be filled up with his love, his goodness, his mercy . . . all sorts of amazing things. And that would be an enormous blessing not just for us but for everyone around us.

My Prayer

Dear God,
Please make my heart hungry for you. Make me thirst for you the way I'd thirst for water in a hot, arid desert. Remind me that I can never get too full of you—and that I need to come to you just as regularly as I head for the lunch line or dinner table.
Amen.

Stone
for the Journey

I am hungry and thirsty for more of God in my life.

Final Word

As the deer pants for streams of water,
so my soul pants for you, O God.

Psalm 42:1 NIV

9

Tender Hearts

Words from the Rock

God blesses those people who are merciful.
They will be treated with mercy!

Matthew 5:7 CEV

How often do you hear someone say, "I don't care"? How often do you say it yourself? Sometimes it seems the world is full of people who simply don't give a rip. But Jesus is saying that you will be blessed when you care—*when you care enough to take care of others*.

Jesus wants you to learn to look outside yourself and see that others are in need. He wants you to learn to put aside your selfishness and roll up your sleeves to help someone else. But do you know why? Is it because God's too busy to take care of everyone? No, of course not. God made the universe—he can easily take care of everyone and everything connected to it. And he does. But his plan is bigger than that. He wants to partner with you.

God knows that you are changed when you help someone else. You grow up a little, and you begin to look more like God. Not only that, but when you care for others, it gets attention. People take notice when someone does something kind or generous or unselfish— because it's a little outside the norm. And when people observe you helping or caring for someone else, they have to scratch their heads and ponder it—like, "What's up with that?" And perhaps someone will be curious enough to ask you—and you can say it's because of God and what he's doing in your life. That'll make 'em wonder.

My Prayer

Dear God,
Teach me to be more caring of others around me. Help me to see when someone is in need. Show me ways I can help. And if anyone asks, let me give the credit to you.
Amen.

Stone
for the Journey

I will keep my eyes peeled for someone who needs my help.

Final Word

> *Love must be sincere. Hate what is evil; cling to what is good.*
>
> Romans 12:9 NIV

10

A Right Heart

Words from the Rock

They are blessed whose thoughts are pure,
for they will see God.

Matthew 5:8 NCV

Jesus said you'll be blessed when your heart, that hidden inner place only God can see, becomes clean and pure. But how do you purify a heart? It's not like you can take Lysol and bleach and give it a good scrub. Even if you could clean it yourself, it would only get dirty again. Because the moment you have bad thoughts toward someone, or feel jealous, or get angry, or lie, or cheat, or hurt someone, your heart gets messed up again. Oh, you can pretend like everything's nice and neat because no one besides you knows just what your heart looks like inside . . . well, except for God. He knows.

And God is the only one who can clean your heart. He did this once and for all by sending his love and forgiveness to earth in the form of Jesus. When you invite Jesus to live in your heart, he's the one who starts cleaning things up. Your job is to cooperate and let him. You can do this by being honest with him, by asking him to help you with areas of your life that need cleaning.

Just as a house needs to be cleaned on a regular basis, so does your heart. It's one of those daily things—a job that must be done again and again. But the good news is that when your heart is clean, you see God in a whole new way—kind of like looking through a freshly cleaned window. And the more you see him, the more you start to look like him.

My Prayer

Dear God,
I invite you to do some deep cleaning inside my heart. I know that you're the only one who can really make my heart pure, and I agree to cooperate. Show me the messy spots I need to turn over to you—and help me allow you to clean them in your own way. I want to see you more clearly. I want to know you better. Thank you!
Amen.

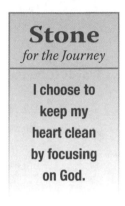

Stone
for the Journey

I choose to keep my heart clean by focusing on God.

Final Word

The purpose of this command is for people to have love, a love that comes from a pure heart and a good conscience and a true faith.

1 Timothy 1:5 NCV

11

Making Peace

Words from the Rock

> *You're blessed when you can show people how to cooperate instead of compete or fight. That's when you discover who you really are, and your place in God's family.*
>
> Matthew 5:9 Message

We hear a lot of talk about world peace—and that's a great goal for everyone to adopt. But how about making peace right where we live? Sometimes the hardest place to keep peace is right under our own roof.

Jesus said that when we learn how to get along peacefully with others, and when we make an effort to help others get along peacefully as well, we begin to experience what being an integral part of God's family is about. Not only that, but people who are watching us can't help but notice that something is different—because all we need to do is look around to see that peace doesn't just happen.

So, next time you sense tension or hear voices rising in anger, say a quick prayer and ask God to lead you, then do your part to encourage cooperation, consideration, understanding—whatever it takes to prevent a fight. Whether it's offering a kind word or a gentle reminder, or simply urging a person to walk away, your efforts will show others that you really are God's child—and you will be blessed.

My Prayer

Dear God,
I confess that sometimes it feels exciting to witness a heated argument—especially if I'm not the one in the middle of it. But I know that's wrong. Please help me be an instrument of peace. Help me remember to place myself in your hands and to be ready to be used for healing instead of hurting.
Amen.

Stone
for the Journey

I will be on the lookout for ways to bring peace to those around me.

Final Word

People who work for peace in a peaceful way plant a good crop of right-living.

James 3:18 NCV

Picked On for God

> *You're blessed when your commitment to God provokes persecution. The persecution drives you even deeper into God's kingdom.*
>
> Matthew 5:10 Message

ecause we live in a country with religious freedom, we don't worry that we might be put to death because of what we believe. And yet there are quiet, subtle forms of persecution that happen fairly regularly. Maybe someone makes fun of you for standing up for your convictions. Or maybe you've been teased for saying a blessing over your lunch or carrying a Bible or attending youth group.

Jesus said you'll be blessed when your faith—that is, your commitment to God—makes others want to persecute you. So perhaps the question is, are you being persecuted because you're doing what God has called you to do? Or are you being persecuted because you're being an in-your-face, Bible-thumping Christian, begging for negative attention? If it's the latter, watch out. That kind of "persecution" won't come with a blessing attached.

Blessing comes as a result of the relationship you have with God. In other words, when you're simply doing what God has asked you to do and, as a result, someone picks on you, God will bless you by increasing his presence in your life. You will feel more connected to him and his kingdom than ever before.

My Prayer

Dear God,
Show me how to serve and love you more. Not in a showy way but in a way that is genuine and humble. And if, while doing that, I get picked on, help me to remember that you are blessing me with more of you and your kingdom. Amen.

Stone
for the Journey

I'll consider it a blessing if I am picked on for my faith.

Final Word

> *Consider it pure joy, my brothers, whenever you face trials of many kinds, because you know that the testing of your faith develops perseverance.*
>
> James 1:2–3 NIV

13

Really Picked On

Words from the Rock

Not only that—count yourselves blessed every time people put you down or throw you out or speak lies about you to discredit me. What it means is that the truth is too close for comfort and they are uncomfortable. You can be glad when that happens—give a cheer, even!—for though they don't like it, I do! And all heaven applauds. And know that you are in good company. My prophets and witnesses have always gotten into this kind of trouble.

Matthew 5:11–12 Message

*N*ow, the sort of persecution Jesus describes in these verses is not the everyday variety. At least not in our country. Jesus was warning his followers that their persecution might be extreme and severe—they would be locked up, tortured, and even executed for their faith. And that's just what happened. Since then, many more generations of Christians have gone through persecution. And in some countries it still happens today.

It's hard to imagine that we could be persecuted for our faith like that in the United States, but if we were, we could be assured that

God would bless us in a huge way. And we could also know that we wouldn't be alone. In a very real sense, we'd have Jesus and all the others who have suffered for their faith standing alongside us, cheering and encouraging us as we remained firm in our commitment to God. Perhaps best of all, we'd know that we really belonged to God—because we'd be enduring the same kind of persecution as his own Son.

My Prayer

Dear God,
It's hard to imagine that the world would ever change so drastically that I would be seriously persecuted for my faith. But if that's ever the case, I pray that you would be my strength and that I would stand firm and remember you are standing right beside me.
Amen.

Stone
for the Journey

I'll hang on tighter to God if the going gets really rough.

Final Word

> *But it is no shame to suffer for being a Christian. Praise God for the privilege of being called by his name!*

1 Peter 4:16 NLT

14

Salty Souls

Words from the Rock

> *You are the salt of the earth. But if the salt loses*
> *its salty taste, it cannot be made salty again. It*
> *is good for nothing, except to be thrown out and*
> *walked on.*
>
> Matthew 5:13 NCV

*W*hen Jesus described his followers as "salt," they probably got it. Or at least they understood that he was saying something good. Although we don't think much of salt today—it's cheap and available everywhere—salt was a highly prized commodity back when Jesus said this. And for his followers to be compared to salt meant they had value too.

I remember a time when my husband's parents were on a salt-free diet. They invited us to dinner, which was some kind of a stew with parsnips and some other vegetables, all without salt. And there was no salt to be had in the house either. That stew was so bland that it was difficult to eat more than a bite or two. In fact, I think I can honestly say it was the worst meal I'd ever eaten. Okay, I'm not crazy about parsnips, but I might've been able to eat them with a bit of salt. That night I realized how valuable salt is.

When Jesus says we're to be salt, it's no small thing. He's saying that our lives, our hearts, our commitment to him should be so savory and flavorful that people will smack their lips and ask for more. Okay, maybe that's stretching the metaphor a bit. But he is saying that he wants us to make a difference. He wants us to be a tasty sample of his love, his forgiveness, his kindness, so that people around us will want seconds.

My Prayer

Dear God,
Help me to be a flavorful sample of what you have to offer for everyone. Show me how to live my life in a way that makes others hungry for you.
Amen.

Stone
for the Journey

I want to add zest and seasoning to the world around me.

Final Word

Be pleasant and hold their interest when you speak the message. Choose your words carefully and be ready to give answers to anyone who asks questions.

Colossians 4:6 CEV

15

Like a Spotlight

Words from the Rock

You are the light of the world. A city on a hill cannot be hidden.

Matthew 5:14 NIV

That's a tall order, isn't it? Jesus said he wants us to be like a bright light that's set on the hilltop of a big city, a beam so bright it can guide people toward the city even when it's pitch black outside. That sounds cool, but what does it mean?

Well, if you know anything about lights, you know that they need something to power them. What good is a flashlight without batteries? What good is a table lamp without electricity? What good is a kerosene lamp without kerosene? I think what Jesus is saying is that we're supposed to be the flashlight or lamp or spotlight, but he will be what powers and fuels the actual light. In other words, it's not up to us to provide the energy to run. We just need to be ready and willing and in the right place at the right time. And we need to be fully connected to him—because even a lamp that's plugged in to a power outlet is useless if it's not turned on. We need his power to flow through us.

So when we say to Jesus, "Here I am; use me however you like," he is able to be that endless power supply that shoots his energy through us, making our lights bright and clear. And that's when people around us will stop and take notice. That light will illuminate things that need to be seen. And who knows, some might even use our light to find their way home—back to God.

My Prayer

Dear God,
I do want to be your light. I want to make myself available to you, connected to you, so that your energy will gush through me and create a light that will help me and others find the way to you.
Amen.

Final Word

He [Jesus] said, "I am the light for the world! Follow me, and you won't be walking in the dark. You will have the light that gives life."

John 8:12 CEV

16

More Light

Words from the Rock

No one would light a lamp and put it under a clay pot. A lamp is placed on a lampstand, where it can give light to everyone in the house. Make your light shine, so that others will see the good that you do and will praise your Father in heaven.

Matthew 5:15–16 CEV

*L*ight is such a great metaphor for how God works. It's no surprise that the Bible uses it over and over. But in these two verses, when Jesus speaks of light, he's bringing it to a whole new level. He's talking about lighting up the home. He starts out by saying that we wouldn't turn on a table lamp, then throw a tarp over it. That would be pretty dumb—not to mention "ungreen" and unsafe.

Jesus is saying that when we're in our homes and living our everyday lives, *we still need to let our light shine.* We still need to remain connected to him and to have his energy flowing through us, because he wants our families, relatives, and close friends to see his light too.

Okay, to be fair, sometimes home is the hardest place to let our light shine. It's easy to want to conceal what God is doing in our lives when we're around parents or siblings—people who have seen the very worst of us, people who might even make fun of us or question our beliefs. But Jesus makes it very clear that he wants us to shine around our family just as much as we shine around others. And he sums it up by saying that when we let our light shine in our homes, the loved ones around us will eventually turn their eyes to God. And, really, what could be better than that?

My Prayer

Dear God,
I confess that sometimes I feel like hiding my faith when I'm at home. And I confess that it's my own family that often brings out the worst in me. Please help me be connected to you, my power source, so I can shine your light in my home. And help those around me see that it's you providing the power!
Amen.

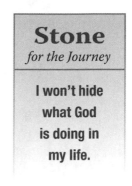

Stone
for the Journey

I won't hide what God is doing in my life.

Final Word

Whatever I say to you in the dark, you must tell in the light. And you must announce from the housetops whatever I have whispered to you.

Matthew 10:27 CEV

17

The Missing Piece

Words from the Rock

Don't suppose for a minute that I have come to demolish the Scriptures—either God's Law or the Prophets. I'm not here to demolish but to complete. I am going to put it all together, pull it all together in a vast panorama.

Matthew 5:17 Message

Some of Jesus's followers had gotten the wrong idea about Jesus. They were so eager for change (political, religious, and personal) that they thought he was going to toss out everything they'd been taught, including God's commandments and Old Testament prophecies, many of which specifically foretold Jesus's life and ministry.

What Jesus wanted them, and everyone, to grasp was that God had a much bigger plan—a plan that had been in place since the beginning of time. Jesus wanted his followers to respect that he was part of God's plan; in fact, he was the most important part. He was like the missing puzzle piece—when he was put into place, they would begin to see the whole picture and get it. And Jesus didn't intend to pull apart all that God had already put together. Instead he was going to do something so amazing (dying on a cross and then rising from the dead) that everything would finally begin to make sense.

It's a lot like that in our lives too. God has put some things together (like who we are, who our parents are, where we live), and he has a purpose in those things. He doesn't want us to toss them aside. But it will take Jesus's involvement in our lives to make that purpose happen. When we partner with him, it's like we finally have the missing pieces to the puzzle, and life actually starts to make sense.

My Prayer

Dear God,
Help me to trust your plans, both for the universe and for my own life. Help me to realize that you've already put some things into place—things I need to accept. And then teach me how to obey and cooperate with you so that my life works out the way you planned it.
Amen.

Stone
for the Journey

I will trust God with the blueprint of my life.

Final Word

> *Trust in the LORD with all your heart*
> *and lean not on your own understanding;*
> *in all your ways acknowledge him,*
> *and he will make your paths straight.*

Proverbs 3:5–6 NIV

18

Law of Love

God's Law is more real and lasting than the stars in the sky and the ground at your feet. Long after stars burn out and earth wears out, God's Law will be alive and working.

Matthew 5:18 Message

God's law may seem big and intimidating, but it's actually pretty simple and straightforward. Despite how religious people have tried to complicate God's law during the past several thousand years, Jesus summed it up in a couple of concise sentences. Here's the nutshell version: (1) Love God. (2) Love your neighbor. Simple, right?

Okay, maybe it's simple, but as you know, simple isn't always easy. Perhaps that's why some religious people try to complicate the law by adding to it and making it tricky—maybe it's a way to distract themselves and others from what God's law really is and from actually doing it.

God's law is simply the ultimate *law of love*. And, as Jesus pointed out, God's law will last forever. So what's the purpose of laws? They are made for us to obey—meaning we have a choice. And not just a onetime choice either—it's a daily choice, sometimes a minute-by-minute choice. And if we choose to love God first of all, wholeheartedly and intentionally, then he will help us to do the next part—to love others (even the unlovable ones). That's how God's law works and how it becomes a living law—and one that lasts forever.

My Prayer

Dear God,
I want to obey your law, but I know I need your help. First, let me choose to love you with all that I am. Then remind me to come to you when I need help in loving others.
Amen.

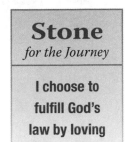

Stone
for the Journey

I choose to fulfill God's law by loving him and others.

Final Word

> Love the Lord your God with all your heart, soul, and mind.
>
> Matthew 22:37 CEV

Take It Seriously

Words from the Rock

> *Trivialize even the smallest item in God's Law and you will only have trivialized yourself. But take it seriously, show the way for others, and you will find honor in the kingdom.*

Matthew 5:19 Message

*I*f you really believe that God's law *is* the law of love, if you truly embrace it and want to obey it, *you need to take it seriously*. But sometimes that's hard. Not everyone is easy to love. Sometimes it would be way easier just to look the other way and pretend like you momentarily forgot that God wants you to love everyone. Or maybe you could cover it up with something else—like a good deed.

But that would be trivializing God's law. It would be like saying, "Hey, God, you didn't really mean it. I don't have to take it seriously . . . no big deal."

Take a moment to think of a person you really don't like—someone you don't even want to love. Maybe it's a sibling who knows how to jab at you when you're already bummed. Maybe it's a bully or a mean girl at school. Maybe there's a certain teacher who doesn't like you, someone who's treated you unfairly. Maybe it's a parent or a grandparent or the next-door neighbor.

And maybe that person has really done you wrong—so much so that you feel justified in your feelings toward them, feelings that have nothing to do with love. That means you are not taking God's law seriously. And it's a putdown to him—and, as a result, it's a putdown to you. You see, you can't slam God without slamming yourself too. That's why he's there, ready to help you to love the most challenging people.

My Prayer

Dear God,
I confess that I have trivialized your law. I know that by not loving [name], I'm not taking you seriously. I know that I'm belittling you, which only makes me a smaller person. Please help me to love everyone. And when I think I can't, please remind me to come to you for help. Amen.

Stone
for the Journey

I will take God seriously and obey his commands.

Final Word

Oh, how I love your law!
I meditate on it all day long.
Your commands make me wiser than my enemies,
for they are ever with me.

Psalm 119:97–98 NIV

20

Keeping It Real

Words from the Rock

Unless you do far better than the Pharisees in the matters of right living, you won't know the first thing about entering the kingdom.

Matthew 5:20 Message

The Pharisees were the religious leaders during Jesus's earthly ministry, and unfortunately, many of them were corrupt. Imagine a really, really bad TV evangelist—he's all dressed up and preaching to his faithful listeners about how God is not happy with them, but if they'll just send him a big fat check, he'll help make things okay between them and God. Yeah, right.

Pretty disgusting, isn't it? But in some ways, that's not a lot different from the Pharisees. It's like they put on a good show, they wore expensive clothes, and they acted a certain way. They probably even seemed to be serving God, but all the while they were making God less accessible than ever before. They pretended to be godly, but underneath their big act, many of them were hypocrites.

That's the last thing Jesus wants to see in us. He doesn't want us to become spiritual hypocrites, falling into the trap of looking good, acting good, saying the right things—while underneath it all we're a mess. Instead, he wants us to remain in a thriving relationship with him. He wants us to be real, not phony. And that's when we experience his kingdom—right here and now!

My Prayer

Dear God,
I don't ever want to be like a Pharisee. Help me to keep it real. Help me to stay close to you so that your life flows through me. And help me to draw people closer to you instead of pushing them away.
Amen.

Stone
for the Journey

**I will honor
God by
being real.**

Final Word

> *Blessed is the man*
> 　　*who does not walk in the counsel of the wicked*
> 　　*or stand in the way of sinners*
> 　　*or sit in the seat of mockers.*
> *But his delight is in the law of the LORD,*
> 　　*and on his law he meditates day and night.*

Psalm 1:1–2 NIV

Watch Your Words

Words from the Rock

You know that our ancestors were told, "Do not murder" and "A murderer must be brought to trial." But I promise you that if you are angry with someone, you will have to stand trial. If you call someone a fool, you will be taken to court. And if you say that someone is worthless, you will be in danger of the fires of hell.

Matthew 5:21–22 CEV

*W*ow, this is a really strong warning about how powerful words can be. Has it ever occurred to you that you can say things that are as lethal as committing murder? Or maybe you've been severely wounded by someone else's thoughtless words toward you. Jesus is commanding you to take the power of your tongue much more seriously. He wants you to understand that wounds from insults and putdowns can sometimes take a lifetime to heal. And some cut so deeply that they can be life threatening.

Think about it. How often have you replayed in your mind something mean that someone has said to or about you? How many times have you felt pain when you remembered some harsh words directed at you? Is it possible that you've inflicted that same kind of pain on someone else? If so, you'd better do whatever it takes to make it right. And although you can't undo the words that were said, you might remember to *think before you speak* next time.

The old adage "If you can't say anything nice, don't say anything at all" may sound trite, but the truth is, it would be much better to keep your mouth shut than to have to stand before Jesus and confess to having murdered someone with your tongue.

My Prayer

Dear God,
Help me to be more careful with my words.
Remind me of the poison that can be slipped into a seemingly small insult. I need your help to control this tongue of mine. Please show me when it's time to keep my mouth shut.
Amen.

Stone
for the Journey

I will control
my tongue
or keep my
mouth shut.

Final Word

> *My tongue will speak of your righteousness*
> *and of your praises all day long.*
>
> Psalm 35:28 NIV

Clean Slate

Words from the Rock

> *This is how I want you to conduct yourself in these matters. If you enter your place of worship and, about to make an offering, you suddenly remember a grudge a friend has against you, abandon your offering, leave immediately, go to this friend and make things right. Then and only then, come back and work things out with God.*
>
> Matthew 5:23–24 Message

*J*esus tells us that we need to keep a clean slate between ourselves and others so that we can avoid hypocrisy. Specifically, he warns that we need to be especially careful when we're going someplace to worship God. Whether it's a Sunday service at church or youth group or a Bible study, we need to make sure we're not taking any unfinished business with us when we're getting ready to praise God with others.

If we attempt to worship, knowing full well that we've offended someone without making it right, we're putting ourselves at serious risk for becoming just like one of those hypocritical Pharisees or that phony-baloney TV evangelist—people who pretend to serve

God but have turned into fakers and takers. Seriously, who wants to end up like that?

Jesus isn't saying that we have to be perfect and somehow manage to live our lives without offending anyone. That's not even possible. What he *is* saying is that we need to make things right with others—we need to say we're sorry and to ask forgiveness—quickly. And especially before we start singing the praises of the one who died on the cross for the very purpose of forgiveness. Then, once the slate is clean, we can come back and worship God without being distracted and without feeling like hypocrites. And, really, isn't that way better?

My Prayer

Dear God,
Help me to remember this important warning.
I want to keep a clean slate with everyone so
I can worship you with honor and truth. Help
me to stay on track.
Amen.

Stone
for the Journey

I will go make things right with others before I go worship God.

Final Word

> Peter came to Jesus and asked, "Lord, how many times shall I forgive my brother when he sins against me? Up to seven times?"
>
> Jesus answered, "I tell you, not seven times, but seventy-seven times."

Matthew 18:21–22 NIV

23

Owning Up

*If your enemy is taking you to court, become
friends quickly, before you go to court. Otherwise,
your enemy might turn you over to the judge, and
the judge might give you to a guard to put you in
jail. I tell you the truth, you will not leave there
until you have paid everything you owe.*

Matthew 5:25–26 NCV

Okay, you probably don't have anyone who's ready to haul you into court, but you never know. What Jesus is saying is that you need to own up to any past wrongs you may have done—back before you were trying to follow Jesus and live according to his rules. (Remember "love God, love your neighbors"?) In the same way you want a clean slate before you go to worship, you want to clear up any past offenses with others as well.

So at any given opportunity, you need to step up and own up. Look that person in the eye and say, "I was wrong, and I am sorry. Please forgive me." And offer to do whatever is necessary to set things right. You just might catch that offended person so off guard that she will simply nod and say, "Okay, no hard feelings."

Do you know why Jesus takes time to say these seemingly basic and obvious things? Because he knows you're human. He knows that you've blown it and that you'll blow it again. But he wants you to clean up your act, so you don't walk around beneath a cloud of guilt and regret and so he can use you to help others. Pretty simple—as long as you cooperate.

My Prayer

Dear God,
Please forgive me for the times I've hurt others. And help me to find the opportunities to make things right. Give me the strength to own up to my messes, to apologize, and to come clean. Amen.

Stone
for the Journey

I will do all I can to restore messed-up relationships.

Final Word

If you have sinned, you should tell each other what you have done. Then you can pray for one another and be healed. The prayer of an innocent person is powerful, and it can help a lot.

James 5:16 CEV

24

Sexual Sin

Words from the Rock

You know the commandment which says, "Be faithful in marriage." But I tell you that if you look at another woman and want her, you are already unfaithful in your thoughts.

Matthew 5:27–28 CEV

Okay, this is a touchy subject (no pun intended) for many people. What was Jesus really saying? Obviously he was talking about sex. And he was stating that sex outside of a marriage relationship is wrong. Nothing new about that. But at the same time he was saying more—much, much more.

He was saying that sexual sin begins long before two people engage in a sexual act. He was saying that when you focus on unmarried sex, when you daydream about it, and when you obsess over it, even if you're not technically having sex, you are still stepping over the line—and you are playing with fire.

Whether it's reading a book that's too graphic, visiting a website that's too skanky, or going too far with your crush, it's wrong. And that's what Jesus was trying to say.

Ironically, this day and age isn't that much different from when Jesus walked the earth. Even then people got caught up in sexual sin. And Jesus knew it was harmful. He knew that it could wound a person's spirit and conscience in a way that nothing else could. He wanted to prevent that. And so he didn't simply say, "Don't have sex outside of marriage." He said, "Don't do all those things that lead up to that." He was basically telling people to protect themselves—and their hearts.

My Prayer

Dear God,
Help me to know where to draw the line. Whether it's in regard to my thought life or to someone I'm dating, please show me what's in my best interest and what's not. And then help me to stay firm in my decision to obey you and put you first in all things.
Amen.

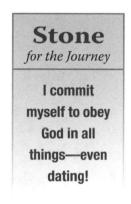

Stone
for the Journey

I commit myself to obey God in all things—even dating!

Final Word

> *Sin pays off with death. But God's gift is eternal life given by Jesus Christ our Lord.*
>
> Romans 6:23 CEV

25

Prevention

Words from the Rock

> *Let's not pretend this is easier than it really is. If you want to live a morally pure life, here's what you have to do: You have to blind your right eye the moment you catch it in a lustful leer. You have to choose to live one-eyed or else be dumped on a moral trash pile. And you have to chop off your right hand the moment you notice it raised threateningly. Better a bloody stump than your entire being discarded for good in the dump.*
>
> Matthew 5:29–30 Message

*U*pon first hearing this, it can seem like a pretty extreme warning. Is Jesus saying we should become blinded or become amputees to avoid sinning? Or is he simply suggesting that we can't blame wrongdoing on a single piece of our lives? That we can't play the victim and pretend that it is an addiction to [fill in the blank] that causes us to sin?

If we selectively blame one thing (especially something outside of our control), we will never own up to the fact that we have the ability to choose between right and wrong. And we will never get better.

So maybe Jesus is being ironic or satiric when he says we should pluck out an eye or cut off a hand to avoid sinning. Maybe what he really means is that we need to get control of ourselves and to admit we're sinful, and then roll up our sleeves to do something about it. Something besides whining and complaining and blaming someone or something else for all our problems. And if we can't handle that, well, maybe we should consider blindfolds and handcuffs first—just to see if they make any difference.

My Prayer

Dear God,
Help me to take control of my life by admitting my weaknesses and confronting my own mistakes. Teach me to make right choices. And most of all, help me to go directly to you for guidance and help.
Amen.

Final Word

> But the Law no longer rules over us. We are like dead people, and it cannot have any power over us. Now we can serve God in a new way by obeying his Spirit, and not in the old way by obeying the written Law.
>
> Romans 7:6 CEV

Stone
for the Journey

I will do whatever I can to avoid making bad choices that hurt me and others.

26

Divorce

Words from the Rock

> *You have been taught that a man who divorces his wife must write out divorce papers for her. But I tell you not to divorce your wife unless she has committed some terrible sexual sin. If you divorce her, you will cause her to be unfaithful, just as any man who marries her is guilty of taking another man's wife.*

> Matthew 5:31–32 CEV

*I*n Jesus's day, there were some men (mostly wealthy ones) who decided they'd grown weary of their wives, and, as a result, they went through the legal, "religious" steps to be free of their wives so they could marry another (maybe a younger, prettier model). Naturally, this practice disgusted Jesus, and he decided to make a statement about it. He took this position not only to put the brakes on divorce in general but for several other good reasons as well.

For one thing, Jesus had real empathy for the cast-off wife because he knew that life could be hard on a divorced woman back then. Without alimony or Social Security, she might end up begging on the streets. But besides that, Jesus knew that everyone related to her would suffer. He knew that divorce would divide a family. He also knew that a "religious" divorce was really a masquerade for hypocrisy. He knew that a line needed to be drawn—and he was willing to draw it.

Does that mean Jesus believed all divorce is wrong? That's not what he was saying. He was only pointing out that some "religious" types were using legal divorce as a cover-up for their own personal sin. He wanted to put a stop to that. In some cases, divorce was the right, just, and kind thing to do—but not usually.

My Prayer

Dear God,
Help me to understand your heart when it comes to confusing issues like divorce and remarriage. Remind me that you are loving and forgiving. But also help me to remember that you want the very best for me and my life. Let me build my life on you and avoid some of these pitfalls that you warn against.
Amen.

Stone
for the Journey

I will strive to do things God's way instead of looking for the easy way out.

Final Word

And so, each of us must give an account to God for what we do. We must stop judging others. We must also make up our minds not to upset anyone's faith.

Romans 14:12–13 CEV

Empty Promises

27

Words from the Rock

And don't say anything you don't mean. This counsel is embedded deep in our traditions. You only make things worse when you lay down a smoke screen of pious talk, saying, "I'll pray for you," and never doing it, or saying, "God be with you," and not meaning it. You don't make your words true by embellishing them with religious lace. In making your speech sound more religious, it becomes less true. Just say "yes" and "no." When you manipulate words to get your own way, you go wrong.

Matthew 5:33–37 Message

Jesus is talking about our words again. He seems to dwell on this a lot—and for good reason. Seriously, isn't it the dumb things we say that get us into the most trouble?

This time Jesus is warning about making promises you don't intend to keep. Or maybe you think you'll keep them, but you can't, because you didn't really consider what you were saying. Maybe you just wanted to sound good, so you made that promise lightly or flippantly—you were blowing hot air. And Jesus says that's wrong.

Do you know why it's wrong? Remember that old hypocrisy thing? Well, when you're standing around in your youth group and you promise to pray for something or someone, sure, you sound like a pretty cool person—a really good Christian. And some might even look up to you because of it. But when you don't really mean it or you don't really do it, aren't you just acting like one of those Pharisees? Aren't you just faking it?

That's why Jesus wants you to keep it simple—and why he says just say yes when you mean it and no when you don't. Jesus doesn't want you to put yourself in a compromising position. The same goes for saying, "God told me to do such and such," when you know it's not true. That's no different than promising something you can't deliver. In other words, it's a lie, and it puts you right back in the hypocrite's chair.

My Prayer

Dear God,
Help me to see that words are crucial—not just to people who hear me speaking but to my own heart as well. Teach me to keep it simple—to say yes when I mean it and no when I don't. Thanks for keeping it simple!
Amen.

Stone
for the Journey

I will say what I mean and mean what I say.

Final Word

> LORD, who may dwell in your sanctuary?
>   Who may live on your holy hill?
> He whose walk is blameless
>   and who does what is righteous,
>   who speaks the truth from his heart.

Psalm 15:1–2 NIV

28

No More Getting Even

Words from the Rock

> *You have heard that it was said, "An eye for an eye, and a tooth for a tooth." But I tell you, don't stand up against an evil person. If someone slaps you on the right cheek, turn to him the other cheek also. If someone wants to sue you in court and take your shirt, let him have your coat also. If someone forces you to go with him one mile, go with him two miles. If a person asks you for something, give it to him. Don't refuse to give to someone who wants to borrow from you.*
>
> Matthew 5:38–42 NCV

It seems to be part of human nature to want justice, fairness, and equality. And while those aren't bad values, we often drag them down and corrupt them. We use them as an excuse for battle. Being human, we get territorial, and we want what's ours. We get mad, and we want others to get what they deserve. Someone lashes out at us, and we want to lash back. It's called *getting even*.

But Jesus changed the rules. He said if someone hits us, we're to stand there and take it. No more hitting back. That's a hard one, isn't it? Everything in us demands our right to defend ourselves—why should we take that kind of abuse from anyone? Surely, we rationalize, Jesus didn't mean this literally.

But what if he did? What if he is telling us to live peacefully simply because he is ready to step in for us? What if he's waiting to be our advocate? What if he has a plan to ultimately make things right for us? Maybe not today, but in his time. What if he just wants us to trust him more?

It takes huge trust to step out of a conflict—especially when we've been wronged. It takes enormous faith to let something go and believe that God will look out for our best interests. And we can do that only when we turn to God and ask for his help. When we find ourselves in tough spots, times when we feel threatened, afraid, or abused—that's when it's time to call out to God. And that's when he steps in and begins to change things and do miracles.

My Prayer

Dear God,
I confess that I don't like being wronged. I want to fight back and defend myself. Please help me to understand that you have a better way. Help me to trust you more and ask for your help when my back is against the wall.
Amen.

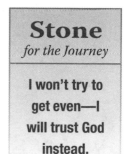

Stone
for the Journey

I won't try to get even—I will trust God instead.

Final Word

Love your enemies and be good to them. Lend without expecting to be paid back. Then you will get a great reward, and you will be the true children of God in heaven. He is good even to people who are unthankful and cruel.

Luke 6:35 CEV

Love Your Enemies

Words from the Rock

You have heard that it was said, "Love your neighbor and hate your enemy." But I tell you: Love your enemies and pray for those who persecute you, that you may be sons of your Father in heaven. He causes his sun to rise on the evil and the good, and sends rain on the righteous and the unrighteous.

Matthew 5:43–45 NIV

Jesus knows that we can relate to loving our friends. Who doesn't love their friends? And for the most part our friends love us back. That's a nice little comfort zone. But Jesus is asking us to step out of our comfort zones. He's telling us that *it's time to love our enemies.* Yikes!

Imagine the person you like the very least, that certain someone you would go out of your way to avoid. Now imagine walking up and throwing your arms around that person and proclaiming your love for him or her. You'd probably both fall over from the shock of it.

Yet Jesus is telling us to love our enemies. He is reminding us that God shares good gifts with all of mankind. Have you ever noticed that when the sun shines, it's not selective about where it sheds its warmth and cheer? Or that on a hot, parched day when the rain finally comes, it will fall on your grumpy neighbor's brown lawn as much as it falls on your own? That's just how God works.

Then Jesus takes us a step further by telling us to pray for people who feel like enemies—people who are mean to us. And maybe that's the best place to start, because something happens to our hearts when we pray for others. *We begin to care.* Of course, Jesus knows this will be the case. He also knows that when we begin to love our enemies, we will begin to look more like God. And he knows that will get people's attention, and, as a result, they might begin to see God in a whole new way.

My Prayer

Dear God,
I confess that I don't want to love my enemies—not really. Teach me to understand the way your love works—how your kindness stretches out toward everyone—and then help me to love others like that.
Amen.

> **Stone**
> *for the Journey*
>
> **I will look for opportunities to show love to and pray for my enemies.**

Final Word

> *Jesus, overhearing, shot back, "Who needs a doctor: the healthy or the sick? Go figure out what this Scripture means: 'I'm after mercy, not religion.' I'm here to invite outsiders, not coddle insiders."*
>
> Matthew 9:12–13 Message

30

Feel the Love

Words from the Rock

If all you do is love the lovable, do you expect a bonus? Anybody can do that. If you simply say hello to those who greet you, do you expect a medal? Any run-of-the-mill sinner does that.

In a word, what I'm saying is, Grow up. You're kingdom subjects. Now live like it. Live out your God-created identity. Live generously and graciously toward others, the way God lives toward you.

Matthew 5:46–48 Message

Okay, this might sound like more of the "love your enemy" commandment, but it's actually different. Jesus is reminding us to *love the unlovely*. But what does that really mean? Because now he's not talking about the people we hate. He's talking more about the people we are uncomfortable with—like people we can't relate to, or shirk away from, or maybe just ignore.

Who is the unlovely person in your life? Perhaps there's more than just one. For starters, that person is probably very different from you—or so you assume. Perhaps he is different ethnically, and you don't understand why he talks or acts the way he does. Or maybe it's a girl who dresses weird. Or a boy who farts in geometry. Or someone who's mentally challenged. Or an elderly person who smells like sauerkraut. Or someone who's unattractive or simply obnoxious. Take your pick.

But Jesus says to love them anyway. He doesn't mince words either. Jesus tells us to "grow up." He points out that it's no big deal to be nice to people who are nice to us. Anyone can do that. But he reminds us once again that we show others that we belong to God when we imitate the way he loves everyone—regardless of how they look, act, talk, or smell!

My Prayer

Dear God,
I confess that I need to learn how to love the kind of people who make me uncomfortable. But I know that I need your help to do this. Please show me someone who I can be kind to today.
Amen.

Final Word

What if I could speak all languages of humans and of angels?

If I did not love others, I would be nothing more than a noisy gong or a clanging cymbal.

1 Corinthians 13:1 CEV

Stone *for the Journey*

I will keep my eyes and heart open for "unlovely" people, and then I will show them God's love at work.

31

All Show, No Go

Be especially careful when you are trying to be good so that you don't make a performance out of it. It might be good theater, but the God who made you won't be applauding.

When you do something for someone else, don't call attention to yourself. You've seen them in action, I'm sure—"playactors" I call them—treating prayer meeting and street corner alike as a stage, acting compassionate as long as someone is watching, playing to the crowds. They get applause, true, but that's all they get.

Matthew 6:1–2 Message

It's no coincidence that Jesus's next warning (after pointing out the good things we should be doing) is a reminder that we need to be sincere and genuine in all we do. Jesus is no fool. He knows there are fakers and takers—people who do acts of goodness for nothing but show and a pat on the back. He describes them as theatrical and hypocritical. They may draw attention to themselves, but God isn't pleased.

Okay, we're only human—and for that reason we all like to be appreciated. It feels good to be approved and even applauded sometimes. But when that becomes our goal, and when we attempt to draw attention to ourselves while serving God, we'd better watch out. When we go around talking about all the amazing things we're doing for God, or when we act more generous, kind, and loving all because we know others are watching . . . well, we might as well forget about it. *God isn't impressed.* For that matter, the people looking on probably aren't either. Oh, they might smile or say, "Good job," but they can probably see right through our little act.

God wants our goodness to come from the heart. He rejoices when we do something for someone else when no one is looking. He loves when we do good deeds secretly—when our only reward is that sweet feeling deep inside ourselves, knowing that God is pleased.

My Prayer

Dear God,
I confess that I do like approval and appreciation. But I don't want that to be my motivation in serving you. Please show me special ways I can do good things for others without drawing attention to myself.
Amen.

Stone
for the Journey

I will be genuine before God and others—he gets the credit, not me.

Final Word

Pure and genuine religion in the sight of God the Father means caring for orphans and widows in their distress and refusing to let the world corrupt you.

James 1:27 NLT

Secret Service

Words from the Rock

*When you help someone out, don't think about
how it looks. Just do it—quietly and unobtrusively.
That is the way your God, who conceived you in
love, working behind the scenes, helps you out.*

Matthew 6:3–4 Message

In a way, Jesus is asking us to join the Secret Service. Okay,
he's not asking us to become underworld spies, but he does
want us to learn how to *serve others secretly*. Do you ever wonder
why that is? Why does he want us to do good deeds without drawing
attention to ourselves? Why does he want us to sneak around to help
others? Why not just let everyone see what we're up to?

The answer is because that's just how God does it. Again and
again, God is quietly at work in our lives—giving us what we need
to live, protecting us from unseen dangers, guiding us through the
maze of our lives . . . and most of the time we don't even notice. And
why does he do it like that? Simply because he loves us. He loves us
so much that he quietly cares for us just like a loving parent. God
doesn't have a rock-star mentality. He doesn't need to make a lot
of noise and expect a standing ovation. Certainly, he's glad when

we do praise and thank him, but that's not why he loves us. He just simply loves us.

And that's what he wants us to learn to do for others: to simply and quietly and unobtrusively love them. So if you see someone in need and you have what it takes to help them, remember you're in the Secret Service, and do it secretly.

My Prayer

Dear God,
Thank you for loving me so much that you take care of me—unobtrusively and without drawing attention to yourself. Help me to learn from you as I attempt to reach out to others in a similar way. Show me opportunities to put your love into quiet action.
Amen.

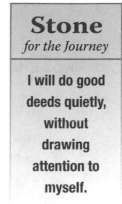

Stone
for the Journey

I will do good deeds quietly, without drawing attention to myself.

Final Word

But among you it will be different. Whoever wants to be a leader among you must be your servant, and whoever wants to be first among you must be the slave of everyone else.

Mark 10:43–44 NLT

33

The Real Deal

And when you come before God, don't turn that into a theatrical production either. All these people making a regular show out of their prayers, hoping for stardom! Do you think God sits in a box seat?

Here's what I want you to do: Find a quiet, secluded place so you won't be tempted to role-play before God. Just be there as simply and honestly as you can manage. The focus will shift from you to God, and you will begin to sense his grace.

Matthew 6:5–6 Message

Once again, Jesus is telling us to *keep it down* and *keep it real*. He's teaching us how to come before God, and he wants us to do it in an appropriate and genuine way. *That means without drama.* Jesus is well aware that some "religious" types like to make a big deal of praying to God. They act like they're starring in *The Ten Commandments* with a packed theater of starstruck fans. They speak loudly and dramatically and put on quite a show. But Jesus says not to.

Instead Jesus gives us a simple plan. He says to find a quiet and private place—a secluded spot where no one is watching. Like a closet. Or maybe your bedroom if you don't share it. Or maybe outside beneath a big old tree. Then you focus on God. Without fanfare or fancy words, you simply be yourself and come before God with all the honesty you can muster.

All he wants is *to be with you* and to have a vital, loving relationship with you. He wants you to converse with him openly, to tell him about your innermost secrets and desires and fears. He wants you to ask him for whatever you need. He wants you to pray for others in your life. And he wants you to be thankful. The best way to communicate with God is to keep it sincere, simple, and straightforward. And if anyone tells you otherwise, you'd better not fall for it.

My Prayer

Dear God,
Thank you for showing me how to come to you. It's a relief to know that I don't need fancy words or dramatic gestures to get your attention. Help me to pray to you as often as possible—and help me to keep it real!
Amen.

Final Word

> *Then if my people who are called by my name will humble themselves and pray and seek my face and turn from their wicked ways, I will hear from heaven and will forgive their sins and restore their land.*

2 Chronicles 7:14 NLT

Stone *for the Journey*

I will look for private places and quiet opportunities to spend time with God.

34

Sweet Simplicity

Words from the Rock

The world is full of so-called prayer warriors who are prayer-ignorant. They're full of formulas and programs and advice, peddling techniques for getting what you want from God. Don't fall for that nonsense. This is your Father you are dealing with, and he knows better than you what you need.

Matthew 6:7–8 Message

The longer we're Christians and around other Christians, the greater the chance that we'll hear about all kinds of tricky techniques for living the "Christian life." We can attend seminars or purchase all sorts of how-to books and CDs and charts and formulas and gadgets and stuff. It's no secret that there's always something new in "Christian" merchandise. That isn't to say that some ideas aren't worthwhile, but in this verse, Jesus reminds us to *keep it simple.*

That's because he doesn't want us to get caught up in a lot of nonsense that might sidetrack us from what's really important—drawing near to God. Jesus saw firsthand how difficult the Pharisees made it for regular people to get close to God. And Jesus doesn't want to see that happen with us.

That's why Jesus warns us that some "prayer techniques" could actually be harmful because they might pull us away from God. He knows our human nature and how we can easily get caught up in fads like "name it and claim it" prayers or "the seven-day prayer plan to a perfect life." And he knows those fads don't really work. Oh, they might seem to at first, but eventually we all need to get back to the basics of keeping it simple.

My Prayer

Dear God,
Help me to understand that praying is simply you and me spending time together in earnest conversation. It's my time to talk with you, to ask you for what I need, to pray for others, to praise you, and to thank you. Sweet and simple. Amen.

Stone
for the Journey

I will keep my prayers sincere and simple—just the way God likes them.

Final Word

When you go without eating, don't try to look gloomy as those show-offs do when they go without eating. I can assure you that they already have their reward.

Matthew 6:16 CEV

35

To the Point

Words from the Rock

You should pray like this:
Our Father in heaven,
help us to honor
your name.
Come and set up
your kingdom,
so that everyone on earth
will obey you,
as you are obeyed
in heaven.
Give us our food for today.
Forgive us for doing wrong,
    as we forgive others.
Keep us from being tempted
    and protect us from evil.

Matthew 6:9–13 CEV

*J*esus wants to make things about prayer perfectly clear. He wants to show us how to get right to the point. And that's why he taught his followers this short, simple, yet all-inclusive prayer. You may have heard it called the Lord's Prayer. And you might even have it memorized in another translation. But what you can't help but notice is that it's very simple and relatively short.

Does Jesus mean that this is the only prayer we should pray, or that we shouldn't expand it or change it? Not at all. He simply wants to show us how prayer is done. He wants to give us some guidelines—something we can both imitate and be inspired by.

Basically, this prayer consists of seven elements. When we pray like Jesus suggests, we acknowledge that (1) God is our heavenly Father, (2) God is in control of heaven, (3) God wants us to obey him on earth, (4) God wants us to ask for our daily needs (like food), (5) God wants us to ask for forgiveness, (6) God wants us to forgive others, and (7) God wants us to ask him for help so we won't be led astray.

This kind of prayer was revolutionary in its simplicity. Unlike the religious leaders of Jesus's day who could go on and on, Jesus got right to the point. And he wants us to do the same.

My Prayer

Dear God,
Thank you for teaching me how to pray. Help me to do it on a regular basis. But help me to keep it personal and real. Remind me that prayer is my lifeline, connecting me directly to you!
Amen.

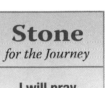

Stone *for the Journey*

I will pray to God on a regular basis.

Final Word

Call to me and I will answer you and tell you great and unsearchable things you do not know.

Jeremiah 33:3 NIV

36

What Goes Around . . .

> *In prayer there is a connection between what God does and what you do. You can't get forgiveness from God, for instance, without also forgiving others. If you refuse to do your part, you cut yourself off from God's part.*
>
> Matthew 6:14–15 Message

esus is making an important point in these two short verses. He wants us to grasp a vital concept—so vital that it's even included in the Lord's Prayer. And yet it's a principle that many Christians struggle to accept.

Jesus puts it right out there, pulling no punches—he states that *we can't be forgiven by God if we refuse to forgive others*. Period. Simple, right? And yet that might be one of the most misunderstood concepts in Christian living. Does the verse mean that God will take away our forgiveness, that he'll undo what Jesus did on the cross, if we don't forgive someone who really, really hurt us? That seems a little harsh, maybe even unfair. Why would a loving, merciful God do that?

But that's where we need to back up. Because it's not God who does that—it's us. When we refuse to forgive someone (no matter how badly we've been hurt), we immediately begin constructing a wall between us and God. And the longer we hang on to our bitterness, the bigger this wall becomes. It's like we add on another stone as each day passes. And finally, the wall is so huge that there is no getting beyond it. But was that wall God's fault? No, of course not. He didn't build it. All he asks is that we imitate him by forgiving others, whether they deserve it or not. And then—with God's help—that wall comes down.

My Prayer

Dear God,
Help me to wrap my head around this. You want me to forgive others so I don't start building a wall that will separate me from you. I don't want to lose out on your forgiveness. I will choose to forgive others as you forgave me. Amen.

Stone
for the Journey

I will forgive others just as God has forgiven me— completely.

Final Word

> *Be kind and compassionate to one another, forgiving each other, just as in Christ God forgave you.*
>
> Ephesians 4:32 NIV

37

Spiritual Show-offs

Words from the Rock

When you practice some appetite-denying discipline to better concentrate on God, don't make a production out of it. It might turn you into a small-time celebrity but it won't make you a saint. If you "go into training" inwardly, act normal outwardly. Shampoo and comb your hair, brush your teeth, wash your face. God doesn't require attention-getting devices. He won't overlook what you are doing; he'll reward you well.

Matthew 6:16–18 Message

Once again, Jesus is warning against showmanship and hypocrisy. Do you wonder why he makes this point so much? Perhaps it's because he understands human nature. Jesus knows that *people like to show off.* And the last way he wants to see anyone showing off is in regard to their relationship with God.

In these verses, Jesus is talking about fasting (the "appetite-denying discipline"). Skipping meals was a popular way for religious people to show their "devotion" to God. Many of them would go around with unwashed bodies and with their heads hanging, acting all pathetic and deprived just so others would notice and be impressed by their "holiness." But as Jesus mentioned before, God wasn't impressed. Neither was Jesus.

Jesus says that if you want to do something like fasting to enhance your spiritual life, go for it—just don't advertise it for the world to see. Otherwise, what's the point? Doesn't it simply turn into a circus with everyone putting on their own sideshow of false spirituality? Who needs that?

My Prayer

Dear God,
Thank you for reminding me again to keep it real. I want to be devoted to you, but not in a way that draws attention to me. Show me how and what I can do to serve you best.
Amen.

> **Stone**
> *for the Journey*
>
> **I will serve God with honesty and devotion.**

Final Word

> *The eyes of the LORD range throughout the earth to strengthen those whose hearts are fully committed to him.*
>
> 2 Chronicles 16:9 NIV

38
Lasting Riches

Words from the Rock

Don't hoard treasure down here where it gets eaten by moths and corroded by rust or—worse!—stolen by burglars. Stockpile treasure in heaven, where it's safe from moth and rust and burglars. It's obvious, isn't it? The place where your treasure is, is the place you will most want to be, and end up being.

Matthew 6:19–21 Message

*I*t's so easy to worry about *things*. It seems to be the American way to be consumed with always "needing" more. Perhaps it's because we live in such a consumer culture—we get bombarded daily by commercial ads that lead us to think that what we have right now is not enough. We need something bigger, better, newer, faster, cooler. But even when we get it, *it's not enough*.

Did you know that one of the most thriving enterprises in our country is the mini storage warehouse—that place where people store their junk after their garages are too stuffed to hold anything else? And then that stuff piled high in the warehouse usually ends up mildewed, ruined by mice or moths, or whatever. What's up with that?

So Jesus reminds us that we need to set our sights much higher than getting the latest, greatest electronic gadget. He says we need to view our spiritual lives and serving him as *the real treasure*. When we do that, it's like having a heavenly bank account. We obey God by loving, forgiving, and helping—and he keeps track. So when we get to heaven, we not only have lots of loved ones to hang with, we have a lasting treasure as well.

My Prayer

Dear God,
Help me to remember that earthly treasures don't last. I want to value what you value—I want to be loving, forgiving, and involved with others. That's where real treasure lies. Help me to find it!
Amen.

Stone
for the Journey

I will treasure what God has in store for me more than material stuff.

Final Word

If you give to others, you will be given a full amount in return. It will be packed down, shaken together, and spilling over into your lap. The way you treat others is the way you will be treated.

Luke 6:38 CEV

Let the Light In

39

Words from the Rock

Your eyes are like a window for your body. When they are good, you have all the light you need. But when your eyes are bad, everything is dark. If the light inside you is dark, you surely are in the dark.

Matthew 6:22–23 CEV

*H*ave you ever noticed how we naturally look toward light? Whether it's a brightly lit sign, a string of colorful Christmas lights, a bonfire, or a full moon, our eyes are drawn to light. Maybe God made us that way to remind us that we need to stay focused on him—his light, his goodness, his loving-kindness—rather than staring into darkness.

Jesus says that our eyes are like windows (or peepholes) that can illuminate our inner lives. But that's only if we keep our eyes opened and focused on God and all his goodness. Then our hearts feel warm and illuminated, and life is good.

But if we focus on things that aren't of God (like self-pity, fear, or hatred), it's as if we've pulled the shades down over our windows. Consequently, our inner self becomes dark and sad and lonely. And if we stay like that too long, it can impair not only how we see things but how we think as well. We need to pull up that shade and get back into the light. That's why Jesus reminds us to keep our eyes lit up by looking at him—since he is, after all, the Light of the World. And when we focus on his goodness, his mercy, and his unconditional love, our hearts are well lit and warm and happy.

My Prayer

Dear God,
I want my eyes to be windows looking straight to you. I want your light to flow through me and to illuminate things I might not otherwise understand. Thank you for filling my heart and my life with your warmth and light.
Amen.

Stone
for the Journey

I will keep my eyes on God, focusing on his goodness and light.

Final Word

> The LORD is my light and my salvation—
>   whom shall I fear?
> The LORD is the stronghold of my life—
>   of whom shall I be afraid?

Psalm 27:1 NIV

40

Choose God

Words from the Rock

No one can serve two masters. The person will hate one master and love the other, or will follow one master and refuse to follow the other. You cannot serve both God and worldly riches.

Matthew 6:24 NCV

This is another pretty strong warning. But you have to appreciate how Jesus gets right to the point. He's not mincing words. He says you can either serve God or serve money. Not both. You can either love God or love money. Not both.

So where does that put you? Do you love money? Do you love God? Now, be honest. Do you want to admit that perhaps you love them both? Okay, sure, you might say that you love God more. But are you certain? Jesus is saying you need to choose. You need to draw the line in the sand and place God on one side, money on the other. Then choose which side you'll take. You can't take both. If you try to, you'll end up hating either God or money. And there's a good chance it would be God. Because, like it or not, money is a powerful force. In some ways, it rules the world. But do you want it to rule your life?

The good news is that if you choose God, you will be taken care of no matter what, because, unlike the mighty dollar, God's resources are limitless. So if you choose him, your resources will be limitless too. Not that he wants you to choose him just because he has deep pockets. No, he wants you to choose him because you really do love him more than money.

My Prayer

Dear God,
I confess that money sometimes seems to have a hold on me. I mean, who doesn't want more? But I choose you, God. I want you, not money, to be my master. I want to love you and put you first in everything.
Amen.

Stone
for the Journey

I choose to serve God first and foremost and put everything else below him.

Final Word

The kingdom of heaven is like what happens when someone finds a treasure hidden in a field and buries it again. A person like that is happy and goes and sells everything in order to buy that field.

Matthew 13:44 CEV

41

No Worries

Words from the Rock

That is why I tell you not to worry about everyday life—whether you have enough food and drink, or enough clothes to wear. Isn't life more than food, and your body more than clothing?

Matthew 6:25 NLT

esus definitely got the big picture. He knew without a doubt that his Father, God, was providing for his every need—big or small, he was covered. No worries. But Jesus also understood that faith like that is not so easy for the rest of us. So he started with simple things, basic things. He said don't worry about food. Don't worry about clothes. There are better ways to spend our time.

Sounds simple—and, really, who likes feeling worried and anxious? But like so many of those other simple-sounding things, it's not always easy to pull it off. For instance, fashion can seem very important sometimes. So important that you might feel anxious about it. And, hey, when you're hungry—you're hungry! But Jesus wasn't saying to just forget about food or clothes or to act like they don't exist. He didn't suggest we run around naked and hungry. All he was saying was *don't worry about them*. Don't get all anxious and fretful and consumed over things like clothes and food. No big deal.

But how do you do that? How do you *not* fret over your clothes when you really want to look cool for a special reason? How do you not feel concerned when you're away from home and broke and starving? You learn to trust God. You learn to *lean on him for everything*. And when you feel anxious about something—whether it's needing a new pair of shoes or it's your growling stomach—tell God what's going on. Ask him to help you. Then see what he can do!

My Prayer

Dear God,
I confess that sometimes it's hard to have faith with everyday things like food and clothes. But I want to trust you more. Remind me to come to you if I feel worried or anxious. I know that you are there to help me. Thanks!
Amen.

Stone
for the Journey

I won't freak over material things— instead I will trust that God will provide.

Final Word

> *For day and night*
> *your hand was heavy upon me;*
> *my strength was sapped*
> *as in the heat of summer.*

Psalm 32:4 NIV

42

Carefree and Cared For

Look at the birds. They don't plant or harvest or store food in barns, for your heavenly Father feeds them. And aren't you far more valuable to him than they are?

Matthew 6:26 NLT

To further make his previous point about not worrying, Jesus tells us to look at the birds. He uses their carefree lives as an example of how we should live. Have you watched birds or listened to them? It seems like they have a pretty good time. They sing happily when they know the sun is coming up. They fly and dart around—sometimes it seems just for the fun of it. Seriously, birds don't have it too bad.

Something else I've noticed about birds is that they are always eating, or snacking, or whatever birds call it. And I'd think they'd run out of food—especially in the heart of winter. Yet they get by just fine. And even on the frostiest day, they still sing as the sun comes up. Even with snow on the ground and food scarce, they still sing and flit and fly like life is good. Why is that?

Because, like Jesus said, they're not worrying about where their next meal is coming from. Somehow God has wired their little bird-brains with the kind of faith that tells them that they'll be okay—there will be food because God will provide. And so they just go about their business—and they have fun while they're doing it. We could learn a lot from the birds.

My Prayer

Dear God,
Okay, sometimes I might feel like a birdbrain, but I admit I don't have a bird's kind of faith. Please help me to trust you more. Help me not to worry about my daily needs. Instead, let me focus on you and all the ways you continue to provide for me. Thank you!
Amen.

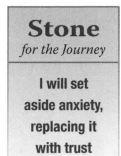

Stone
for the Journey

I will set aside anxiety, replacing it with trust and faith.

Final Word

When that time comes, you won't have to ask me about anything. I tell you for certain that the Father will give you whatever you ask for in my name.

John 16:23 CEV

43

Just Relax

Words from the Rock

Has anyone by fussing in front of the mirror ever gotten taller by so much as an inch? All this time and money wasted on fashion—do you think it makes that much difference? Instead of looking at the fashions, walk out into the fields and look at the wildflowers. They never primp or shop, but have you ever seen color and design quite like it? The ten best-dressed men and women in the country look shabby alongside them. If God gives such attention to the appearance of wildflowers—most of which are never even seen—don't you think he'll attend to you, take pride in you, do his best for you?

Matthew 6:27–30 Message

*D*o you suppose there's a reason Jesus continues to talk about not worrying? Do you think he suspects it might take hearing all this a time or two, or ten thousand, before you get it?

This time he's talking about flowers and how lovely they look—delicate wildflowers, which are sometimes here today and gone tomorrow. Yet he describes them as if they were royalty. Then he points out that you are much more important to God than flowers. So why wouldn't God want you to look great too? That's kind of reassuring. Especially if you like looking nice. You see, God wants you to look nice too!

But here's the deal. He doesn't want you to obsess over your looks. He doesn't want you to fret over your clothing. He doesn't want you to stay up late at night trying to decide what to wear the next day. He wants you to just relax. Give yourself a break. Instead of worrying, why not spend time with God? Why not tell him about what's troubling you and ask for his advice? He might even have a fashion tip or two to share. The main thing is to quit worrying. Worrying won't change anything. Give your cares and concerns to God, and who knows? Maybe you'll avoid a few worry wrinkles or frown lines.

My Prayer

Dear God,
I admit that I do worry about my appearance and how I'm dressed. But I want to let it go. I want to just relax. And to do that, I know I have to trust you. Show me how to turn my cares over to you. Thanks!
Amen.

> **Stone**
> *for the Journey*
>
> **I will trust God to give me what I need—even when it comes to clothes.**

Final Word

> *I will lie down and sleep in peace,*
> *for you alone, O Lᴏʀᴅ,*
> *make me dwell in safety.*

> Psalm 4:8 NIV

44

Hang with God

Words from the Rock

What I'm trying to do here is to get you to relax, to not be so preoccupied with getting, so you can respond to God's giving. People who don't know God and the way he works fuss over these things, but you know both God and how he works. Steep your life in God-reality, God-initiative, God-provisions. Don't worry about missing out. You'll find all your everyday human concerns will be met.

Matthew 6:31–33 Message

More than anything, Jesus wants you to get connected to God. He wants you to know God intimately and to love God completely—just like Jesus does. He says that if you didn't know God, you'd have reason to be worried. But because you do know God, you should know that he is caring for you. And for that reason, you shouldn't be concerned about having what you need. God will provide!

But maybe you're still wondering, *How do I get to know God?* The answer is: the same way you get to know anyone. Say you meet a guy that you really like, but you don't really know him—what do you do? Assuming this guy likes you too, you would probably begin spending time together. You would talk and do things together, and before long you would know each other.

It's no different with God. You spend time with him. You talk to him. You listen. You tell him your secrets. You find out his likes and dislikes. You begin to care about the same things he cares about. In time, you and God are best friends, and you wonder how you ever got along without him. And guess what? While you're doing all this—focusing your attention and energy on getting to know God—he is quietly taking care of everything you need.

My Prayer

Dear God,
I know that I need to know you better. Show me how I can spend more time with you. Help me to talk to you openly, even in those moments when I think I don't want to. Thank you for taking care of all that I need.
Amen.

> **Stone**
> *for the Journey*
>
> **I will spend time with God, knowing that he is taking care of what I need.**

Final Word

I will bless you with a future filled with hope—a future of success, not of suffering.

Jeremiah 29:11 CEV

45

Here and Now

Words from the Rock

Give your entire attention to what God is doing right now, and don't get worked up about what may or may not happen tomorrow. God will help you deal with whatever hard things come up when the time comes.

Matthew 6:34 Message

This is one of my all-time favorite Rock verses. Honestly, I could just about build my whole life on this one. This is a fairly short and succinct Bible verse, but in it Jesus tells us three extremely important things. First of all, he says to *give God our full attention*. He doesn't say it's okay to do it later—he says to do it RIGHT NOW. And that means do it ALWAYS and every day. Get it? Does it get any clearer?

Second, Jesus tells us not to freak over tomorrow or what we think may or may not happen. In other words, *don't worry*, don't be anxious, and don't stress over things that haven't even happened yet. *Okay*, you might be thinking, *that's easier said than done.* How does a person go about doing that? How is it possible NOT to worry? Especially if your life, like most people's, doesn't travel down a nice, smooth road.

And that's where the third part of this verse comes in handy. Jesus tells us that *God will help us handle whatever tough stuff comes.* And since this is life on earth (not heaven), we can plan on plenty of hard things heading our way. But Jesus's promise is that when we need it, when the time comes, God will help us. We just need to believe him, have faith, stand on the Rock, and trust that he can do it.

My Prayer

Dear God,
You are my Rock. Help me to keep my eyes on you, not tomorrow or next week, but RIGHT NOW. And help me not to worry about what's going to happen next but believe that you are going to help me handle whatever life sends my way—because you are my Rock, and I can trust in you!
Amen.

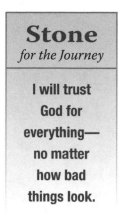

Stone
for the Journey

I will trust God for everything— no matter how bad things look.

Final Word

I've commanded you to be strong and brave. Don't ever be afraid or discouraged! I am the LORD your God, and I will be there to help you wherever you go.

Joshua 1:9 CEV

46

Don't Judge

Do not judge others, and you will not be judged.
For you will be treated as you treat others. The
standard you use in judging is the standard by
which you will be judged.

Matthew 7:1–2 NLT

This is probably one of the most explicit and to-the-point statements that Jesus ever made. And, like many of his other important teachings, he didn't speak about judgment only once. He made this same point numerous times—and always with passion. Not only that, but he lived out this teaching in his actions and choices—often taking flak from religious leaders as a result. It's like he wanted to ensure there was no wiggle room in his words. He wanted us to get it!

And yet judging others is something that many Christians do. In fact, there are many nonbelievers who feel that Christians are among the most judgmental people on the planet. Can you imagine how that must make Jesus feel? Here we are, the people who bear his name by claiming to be Christians, and yet sometimes we throw his words right back in his face by choosing to judge or criticize or put down others.

Why is that? Where does judgment come from? Maybe you've heard the old quote, "Don't criticize someone until you've walked a mile in his moccasins"—meaning we don't know what other people go through because we're not them. Ignorance is often the source of judgment. Let's say there's a guy at school who walks around like Mr. Snooty and seems so full of himself. But what if he's been really hurt by someone? What if he's wearing superiority like a protective overcoat to keep from being hurt again? If you assume he's just stuck-up, you are guilty of both ignorance and judgment. So wise up and try to understand others on a deeper level—and see if your judgments don't slowly evaporate.

My Prayer

Dear God,
Help me look beneath the rough exteriors of others. Help me to get rid of my ignorance and to see people as you see them.
Amen.

Final Word

We must stop judging others. We must also make up our minds not to upset anyone's faith.

Romans 14:13 CEV

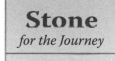

Stone
for the Journey

Judging or criticizing others only reveals my own ignorance.

47

Hypocritical "Help"

Words from the Rock

> *Why do you look at the speck of sawdust in your brother's eye and pay no attention to the plank in your own eye? How can you say to your brother, "Let me take the speck out of your eye," when all the time there is a plank in your own eye? You hypocrite, first take the plank out of your own eye, and then you will see clearly to remove the speck from your brother's eye.*
>
> Matthew 7:3–5 NIV

*O*nce again, Jesus is warning against hypocrisy as well as judgment. Only this time he's exposing a tendency to disguise insincere opinions as helpfulness. Obviously he has reasons for making this point. He knows that humans, being flawed, might try to invent ways to appear innocent while annihilating others.

Say you have an overweight friend who's struggling to stay on her diet. Maybe she's even asked for your help. So you walk into the cafeteria and catch her snarfing down some fries, so you say something "helpful" like, "Hey, if you don't want to be a cow, why are you eating like a pig?" So maybe she gets mad and tosses the fries in the trash, then stomps out. And you hold your hands up like, "What did I do? She said she wanted my help."

The point is, that wasn't helpful. It was hurtful. And even if she has a problem with what she's putting into her mouth, you might have a problem with what's coming out of yours. And, really, which is worse? Her choice to fudge on her diet hurts only her. But your choice to say something mean is hurtful and humiliating and wrong. Your "helpfulness" will probably make your friend's problem worse, plus you'll end up looking like a jerk. And how does that make God look?

My Prayer

Dear God,
I sometimes do or say things in the pretense of helpfulness, but I know in my heart that they aren't helpful. Teach me to help others from motives that are pure. Show me ways to encourage others through kindness and love. Amen.

Final Word

> Some of you accuse others of doing wrong. But there is no excuse for what you do. When you judge others, you condemn yourselves, because you are guilty of doing the very same things.
>
> Romans 2:1 CEV

Stone
for the Journey

I will examine my own heart—and my own motives—before I attempt to straighten out someone else.

48

Guard Your Heart

Words from the Rock

> *Don't give to dogs what belongs to God. They will*
> *only turn and attack you. Don't throw pearls down*
> *in front of pigs. They will trample all over them.*
>
> Matthew 7:6 CEV

The translation of the Greek for this Scripture is basically, "Don't give the sacred to the dogs." That might not make much sense in itself, at least in our culture. But in Jesus's time, dogs and pigs were pretty low on the animal importance scale. Dogs were more like scavengers than pets. And pigs were considered "unclean"— not an animal a Jewish person would own. So what is Jesus saying?

I think he's warning us to protect our hearts by not going around and telling anyone and everyone about what God is doing in our lives. Sure, there are times when God wants you to share your faith with others—and often he'll make it clear when it's the right time. But there are other times when you might be tempted to tell someone (a person who couldn't care less about God or faith or even you) about something important and miraculous that God is doing in your life. And that person might, in effect, spit on what you're saying. He might argue with you or put down God. And, in the end, not only does it make you feel sad, but it's also useless since the person obviously doesn't get it. It's like taking a diamond ring and flushing it down the toilet. Pointless and wasteful.

God wants you to value what he's doing in your heart and in your life. He wants you to treat his words and his work in you as something precious and wonderful—and not to toss them around lightly.

My Prayer

Dear God,
I know you're at work in me. You're doing some amazing things in my heart. Give me the wisdom to know when it's best to keep these things to myself and when it's okay to tell others.
Amen.

Final Word

Be prepared. You're up against far more than you can handle on your own. Take all the help you can get, every weapon God has issued, so that when it's all over but the shouting you'll still be on your feet.

Ephesians 6:13 Message

Stone
for the Journey

I will treasure God's work in my life so much that I won't flippantly show off my spirituality to others.

Prayer Promises

Words from the Rock

Ask, and it will be given to you; seek, and you will find; knock, and it will be opened to you. For everyone who asks receives, and he who seeks finds, and to him who knocks it will be opened.

Matthew 7:7–8 NASB

Jesus makes us an incredible promise in these verses. In fact, this promise sounds almost too good to be true. And yet it is totally legit—we just need to have the faith to believe and embrace it. But most of all, we need to really wrap our heads and hearts around it. It takes some insight to fully grasp and understand what this promise actually means. Unfortunately, a common human response is to assume that this verse is the "magic formula." That if you simply pray those words—presto chango—you should get whatever it is you want. Kind of like a genie lamp, right? Wrong.

For starters, Jesus isn't promising he'll give us material things like money or cars or designer shoes, and he's not even saying he'll hand over desired things like success or romance. He's primarily talking about the most important elements in life. In other words, he's saying that when we seek him out and ask him to meet our spiritual needs, he will absolutely deliver the goods—*the spiritual goods.*

Oh, he might not deliver exactly what we expect. Say we pray for patience, and all we get are more challenges (which eventually teach us patience). Also, God's timing often differs from ours (we usually think in terms of fast food—here and now!), and sometimes he says, "Later." But when we knock on spiritual doors, when we ask Jesus to meet us, and when we seek God's guidance—doors will open, Jesus will be there, and we will definitely receive. We can count on it!

My Prayer

Dear God,
Show me how to seek you more, to knock on more doors, and to expect some life-changing answers from you.
Amen.

Final Word

He will give us whatever we ask, because we obey him and do what pleases him.

1 John 3:22 CEV

Stone
for the Journey

I will ask and seek and knock with the expectation that God will answer.

50

Our Provider

Words from the Rock

You parents—if your children ask for a loaf of bread, do you give them a stone instead? Or if they ask for a fish, do you give them a snake? Of course not! So if you sinful people know how to give good gifts to your children, how much more will your heavenly Father give good gifts to those who ask him.

Matthew 7:9–11 NLT

It might not always seem like it, especially to a teenager, but most parents want the best for their kids. They want to give them nice things and make sure all their needs are met. That's just part of being a good parent. And even when parents have to sacrifice to provide, they're usually glad to do it—because they love their kids. And yet these are earthly parents, and they are just human—and, as you probably know, they are not perfect.

But God, on the other hand, is perfect. And he is the most loving parent in the universe. So loving, in fact, that he provides abundantly for all his creation—whether they believe in him or not. He's designed the planet to provide our basic needs (like food, water, oxygen, and sunlight), as well as making it extremely scenic with beautiful sights (like lakes, oceans, mountains, and forests) for our pleasure and enjoyment.

And that's just the beginning. Because there is much more that he is ready to share. He has life-impacting gifts (like peace, joy, and love) that he wants to pour on us. Our heavenly Father is able to do much more than what any earthly parent can dream of. But he needs us to be ready—*ready to receive.* Jesus is trying to help us grasp this concept—to understand that God, the perfect and loving heavenly Father, is ready to give every good and perfect gift to us. But first he wants us to come to him—and ask.

My Prayer

Dear God,
Help me to understand how much you love me. Help me to come to you for all my needs, knowing that you want to give only the very best to me.
Amen.

Final Word

Stone
for the Journey

My heavenly Father is ready to give me more good things than I can begin to imagine.

> Our LORD and our God,
> you are like the sun
> and also like a shield.
> You treat us with kindness
> and with honor,
> never denying any good thing
> to those who live right.
>
> Psalm 84:11 CEV

51

Getting Along

Words from the Rock

*Treat others as you want them to treat you. This is
what the Law and the Prophets are all about.*

Matthew 7:12 CEV

*Y*ou might have heard this often-quoted Scripture called
the Golden Rule before. Maybe you recall a version like
this: "Do unto others as you would have them do unto you." Perhaps
your third grade teacher posted it on the bulletin board to remind
kids to be nice. And if you had to choose only one rule for interacting
with others, this would be an excellent one.

Perhaps the most mind-boggling thing about this rule is that it's
so simple. Of course, just because it's simple doesn't mean it's easy.
But it's nothing short of amazing that Jesus is able to sum up, in
one sentence, what generations of Jewish scribes and Pharisees had
taken thousands of years and thousands of words to explain. They had
made lists and lists of cumbersome laws and rules and sacrifices and
atonements—yet they never really got it. It's like they were incapable
of treating others with the respect they demanded for themselves.
Instead of exhibiting kindness and love, they focused on outward
legalities to force people into "good behavior." But Jesus focuses on
the heart—when the heart changes, good actions simply follow.

Jesus says to treat others the way you want to be treated—period. If you want to be respected, show some respect. If you want to be loved, love others. If you want people to share with you, be generous toward them. In other words, whatever it is that you feel you're not getting, try giving it first. Then see what happens.

My Prayer

Dear God,
Remind me that my own needs and wants are like a mirror, reflecting what it is that I should be giving to others. Show me new ways to do this.
Amen.

Stone
for the Journey

I will treat others how I want to be treated.

Final Word

For the whole Law is fulfilled in one word, in the statement, "You shall love your neighbor as yourself."

Galatians 5:14 NASB

One Way

Words from the Rock

Go in through the narrow gate. The gate to destruction is wide, and the road that leads there is easy to follow. A lot of people go through that gate. But the gate to life is very narrow. The road that leads there is so hard to follow that only a few people find it.

Matthew 7:13–14 CEV

Some people assume that when Jesus teaches about the "narrow gate," he is talking only about what happens after you die. But Jesus had made it clear right from the start that he came to bring life—here and now—and he came to make our earthly lives bigger and better than they've ever been before. And yet, he says, we have to go through a narrow gate. So what does that mean?

In other Scriptures, Jesus is called "the door" and "the way." As you can see, both these metaphors are similar to a gate in that they are types of entryways. That's because Jesus is the entrance to God. He's the guy who welcomes us with arms outspread, saying, "Come on in!" He's our living invitation to enter into God's kingdom—not after we're dead but right here in this very life. He wants us to experience all the wonders and gifts and satisfaction of God's kingdom right here on earth. And he's not only our ticket, he's the gateway to enter.

Does that suggest that Jesus is "narrow" or "small" or "tight"? Or is he simply comparing his very specific entryway to the thousands of other "options" out there? Unbelievers will say things like, "Do whatever feels good," "Any way is the right way," "It's all relative," "There are no absolutes," or "Hey, whatever." But Jesus, in essence, says, "Come through my gate. It might seem harder to get through initially, but it'll be so worth it!" And, seriously, think about it. Which road sounds more interesting—a narrow, winding mountain path that weaves past trees and rivers and fields and waterfalls, leading up to the summit, or a long, wide asphalt highway that goes straight and flat and leads nowhere?

My Prayer

Dear God,
Help me to continually choose Jesus as my entrance to you. And if the path seems hard or challenging, remind me where that flat highway goes.
Amen.

Final Word

Work hard to enter the narrow door to God's Kingdom, for many will try to enter but will fail.

Luke 13:24 NLT

Stone
for the Journey

My real life begins when I enter it through Jesus—he is my gateway to fulfillment.

53

Beware

> *Be wary of false preachers who smile a lot, dripping with practiced sincerity. Chances are they are out to rip you off some way or other. Don't be impressed with charisma; look for character. Who preachers are is the main thing, not what they say. A genuine leader will never exploit your emotions or your pocketbook. These diseased trees with their bad apples are going to be chopped down and burned.*
>
> Matthew 7:15–20 Message

Jesus, being one with God and supernatural, knew that lots of false teachers and preachers would come after his earthly ministry ended. He knew that many would attempt to lead people astray in "the name of Jesus." Whether they did it for money or prestige or power, or simply because they were mixed up, Jesus knew that those teachers and preachers would be around for a long time. Just like he predicted, there were many that came shortly after his death and resurrection. And now, more than two thousand years later, they're still around.

But how do you know whether a spiritual leader is the real deal? Unfortunately, it's not always easy to figure out—at first. Most false preachers have natural charm and charisma. They have the kind of traits that draw people in. They seem well spoken and smart. They appear to be warm and friendly and personable—just like a legitimate preacher. So how do you know who's who?

For one thing, a false teacher or preacher places a lot of focus on money—particularly yours. Too much pressure to give financially is not a good sign. Also, a false teacher might jerk you around emotionally, pushing you to places far beyond your comfort zone and not even healthy. Also, they may have a bad track record—a history of hurting others, moving around a lot, broken marriages, money problems. All are signs that something's wrong. Does that mean preachers and teachers can't make mistakes? Of course not. Everyone makes mistakes. But a legitimate leader will admit his failures and change his ways. A false leader won't.

My Prayer

Dear God,
Please help me to know the difference between a false leader and someone who truly loves and serves you. Help me to be part of a healthy church.
Amen.

Final Word

Dear friends, do not believe everyone who claims to speak by the Spirit. You must test them to see if the spirit they have comes from God. For there are many false prophets in the world.

1 John 4:1 NLT

Stone *for the Journey*

Don't be so impressed with outward appearances that you miss what lies beneath.

54

Authentic Faith

> *Not everyone who calls me their Lord will get into the kingdom of heaven. Only the ones who obey my Father in heaven will get in. On the day of judgment many will call me their Lord. They will say, "We preached in your name, and in your name we forced out demons and worked many miracles." But I will tell them, "I will have nothing to do with you! Get out of my sight, you evil people!"*
>
> Matthew 7:21–23 CEV

These passionate and angry words of Jesus come directly after what he says about false teachers and fake preachers and lying prophets. Can you understand why Jesus would be so aggravated and irritated at people who were passing themselves off as his servants in order to take advantage of others? Why wouldn't he be enraged?

Imagine how you would feel if someone pretended to be your good friend in order to rip off some poor, innocent person who knew and trusted you. What would you do if the victim came to you in tears and said, "Why did you send that thief to my house? Why did you tell that rapist to introduce himself as your friend?" You'd be shocked and sorry and probably furious. That's what Jesus's reaction will be to anyone who uses his name as a pretense to falsely "minister" to others while picking their pockets. And unless they have confessed their sins and repented, those predators and spiritual fakes will not be welcome in heaven.

Jesus states that only the ones who "obey my Father" will be allowed into heaven. A strong warning, to be sure, but Jesus has strong feelings about those who would fake their ministry and use his name not only to cheat his followers out of money, but also to cheat them out of experiencing things like love, joy, peace, honesty, happiness, and all the spiritual fruits that would be the result of a legitimate ministry.

My Prayer

Dear God,
Help me to always obey you so I'll never be accused of being a false anything. And help me to be quick to sniff out any false leaders who might be attempting to recruit me.
Amen.

Final Word

Depart from me, all you workers of evil,
for the LORD has heard the sound of my weeping.

Psalm 6:8 ESV

> **Stone**
> *for the Journey*
>
> **Just because someone claims to serve God does not mean they do.**

55

Rock Solid

Words from the Rock

Anyone who listens to my teaching and follows it is wise, like a person who builds a house on solid rock. Though the rain comes in torrents and the floodwaters rise and the winds beat against that house, it won't collapse because it is built on bedrock. But anyone who hears my teaching and doesn't obey it is foolish, like a person who builds a house on sand. When the rains and floods come and the winds beat against that house, it will collapse with a mighty crash.

Matthew 7:24–27 NLT

*J*esus didn't have TV or movies to assist in his teachings, but he did know how to create vivid images—ones that would remain indelibly printed on the minds of millions over the next two thousand years—through his gift of storytelling. And this particular parable (meaning a story with a lesson) is a great visual aid for understanding how Jesus is our rock-solid foundation.

Everyone likes the idea of a beach house, right? Imagine these two surfer dudes who decide to build their seaside dream homes. One guy can't wait to get into his house—he's imagining something very cool and something great for parties, and he wants it done fast. So he buys the cheapest ocean-view lot and quickly builds his dream home right on the sand near the water. But the other guy does some research and pays more money to buy a lot a little higher—same great view, but the lot is on stone, and the house doesn't go up as quickly since it takes time to do things right. Finally both houses are complete—and then a hurricane hits. Guess which guy is suddenly homeless?

That's how people feel when their lives aren't built on Jesus. He's the Rock that anchors us through the worst storms—and they do come eventually. Sure, it might seem faster or easier to just plant a house on the beach and kick back, but that house won't get us through the storms. Jesus, the Rock, will.

My Prayer

Dear God,
I want my life to be firmly grounded on you.
Help me to hold fast to your truth and your words so my "house" will withstand the worst of storms.
Amen.

Final Word

> Live under the protection
> of God Most High
> and stay in the shadow
> of God All-Powerful.
> Then you will say to the LORD,
> "You are my fortress,
> my place of safety;
> you are my God,
> and I trust you."

Psalm 91:1–2 CEV

Stone
for the Journey

Only a rock-solid foundation on Jesus will keep you safe during life's hurricanes.

56

Priorities

> *Another disciple said to Jesus, "Lord, let me wait*
> *till I bury my father." Jesus answered, "Come with*
> *me, and let the dead bury their dead."*
>
> Matthew 8:21–22 CEV

*I*n Jewish tradition, there was almost nothing that took precedence over the death of a loved one. And although the body was buried quickly, sometimes it took several days to handle the responsibilities of seeing to the widow, the inheritance, and other details. Under normal circumstances, a devoted son wouldn't dream of taking off during that time. In fact, his friends and neighbors would probably label him as a no-good loser if he did such a thing.

But Jesus, the Messiah, was inviting this man to *follow* him. Jesus was offering him the privilege to come and listen and learn from the Son of God. This was an opportunity that came around, well, only once in eternity. Others had left jobs, spouses, children, families, neighbors, and livelihoods in order to follow Jesus during his brief earthly ministry. And you can bet that none of them regretted their choice when all was said and done.

When Jesus said, "Let the dead bury their dead," he was in essence saying, "Come and experience life." If that man had gone with

Jesus, if he'd taken the time to discover what Jesus had to offer, he could have eventually gone back to his family (who were spiritually dead) and shared Jesus's words of life with them. But he declined the invitation.

The good news is that Jesus extends this invitation to everyone. He invites you to step away from the land of the dead and to experience the fullness of life.

My Prayer

> Dear God,
> Thank you for the opportunity of a lifetime—
> to follow you and to live my life to the fullest.
> Help me to always choose life over death.
> Amen.

Stone
for the Journey

Saying no to Jesus is like climbing into a casket and closing the lid.

Final Word

> *Jesus said to him, "Come with me!" So he got up and went with Jesus.*
>
> Mark 2:14 CEV

57

No-Fear Faith

After Jesus left in a boat with his disciples, a terrible storm suddenly struck the lake, and waves started splashing into their boat. Jesus was sound asleep, so the disciples went over to him and woke him up. They said, "Lord, save us! We're going to drown!" But Jesus replied, "Why are you so afraid? You surely don't have much faith." Then he got up and ordered the wind and the waves to calm down. And everything was calm. The men in the boat were amazed and said, "Who is this? Even the wind and the waves obey him."

Matthew 8:23–27 CEV

*M*ost people would freak if they were in a small boat out in the middle of the sea and a big squall began. Think about it. The sky grows dark with clouds, the rain comes down in a cold deluge, the wind whips up waves that are taller than the boat, and—this is a big one—you know you're going down. Who wouldn't be scared?

Well, everyone would be—except Jesus, that is. Jesus was sleeping soundly in the boat. The disciples, certain they were doomed, felt they had to wake him. But what do you suppose would've happened if they hadn't awakened him? Would the boat have sunk and everyone in it have drowned at sea? (So much for God's plan to save the world.) Of course not. And that's exactly why Jesus was able to sleep. He knew they were going to be just fine. That's also probably why he was slightly aggravated at his disciples for waking him. And that's probably why he reprimanded them by saying, "Why are you so afraid? You surely don't have much faith."

They had already seen Jesus perform all kinds of miracles—up close and personal. They already knew him well, and they knew that he had come from God. And yet their faith was small. What hope is there for us?

The hope comes later, when Jesus empowers them and us by sending the Holy Spirit to help us, to guide us, and to remind us (again and again) that God knows what he's up to. And if we're where we should be (even in a huge storm), God will keep us safe.

My Prayer

Dear God,
Help my faith to grow stronger. Remind me that you really are in control and that as long as I'm leaning on you, I'll be fine.
Amen.

Final Word

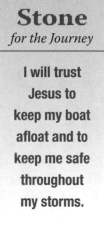

Stone
for the Journey

I will trust Jesus to keep my boat afloat and to keep me safe throughout my storms.

If you have faith the size of a mustard seed, you will say to this mountain, "Move from here to there," and it will move; and nothing will be impossible to you.

Matthew 17:20 NASB

58

Power to Forgive

Words from the Rock

"Take courage, son; your sins are forgiven. . . .
"Which is easier, to say, 'Your sins are forgiven,'
or to say, 'Get up, and walk'? But so that you may
know that the Son of Man has authority on earth
to forgive sins"—then He said to the paralytic, "Get
up, pick up your bed and go home."

Matthew 9:2, 5–6 NASB

*W*ord of Jesus's incredible ministry spread quickly, and more people came to him, hoping for miracles. This was the case when he arrived in his hometown and a paralyzed man was brought to him for healing. But when Jesus bent down and kindly told the sick man that his sins were forgiven, some of the Jewish leaders took offense. In their opinion, forgiveness wasn't something a person could just hand out. According to their laws, it had to be purchased.

Jesus knew what they were thinking (and saying behind his back), so he used this opportunity to make an important point. He made it clear that not only did he have the authority to forgive sins, but he also had the power to heal. And this authority and power came from the same source—his Father God. Now, it was one thing for the religious leaders to be upset when Jesus forgave someone's sins, but can you imagine how shocked they must've been when Jesus healed that paralyzed man?

But Jesus wasn't simply showcasing God's authority that day. Maybe that's why he linked the power of forgiveness with the miracle of healing. Today, more than two thousand years later, medical professionals are admitting that forgiveness and physical and emotional wellness go hand in hand. In other words, if we reject forgiveness, our bodies and minds will probably suffer for it.

My Prayer

Dear God,
Remind me that I need to experience your forgiveness on an ongoing basis. Help me to see how it impacts all areas of my life—including my health and wholeness.
Amen.

Stone
for the Journey

Jesus's forgiveness is vital to my physical and emotional health.

Final Word

And he has given him the authority, simply because he is the Son of Man, to decide and carry out matters of Judgment.

John 5:27 Message

Needy Hearts

Words from the Rock

Healthy people don't need a doctor—sick people do. . . . Now go and learn the meaning of this Scripture: "I want you to show mercy, not offer sacrifices." For I have come to call not those who think they are righteous, but those who know they are sinners.

Matthew 9:12–13 NLT

Shortly after healing the paralyzed man, Jesus met a tax collector named Matthew who later invited Jesus to dine at his house. Now to get this, you have to understand that tax collectors were like the bottom-feeders in Jewish society. In fact, they weren't much different from thieves, since they collected exorbitant taxes from the locals, then pocketed the profits from their take before handing the remainder over to the oppressive Roman government. In other words, they got rich at the expense of their neighbors.

When the local religious leaders (the same ones who complained about Jesus's forgiveness) observed Jesus going to dine with this low-life tax collector, they were shocked. And if Matthew wasn't scandalous enough, didn't Jesus realize that that crook hung out with other thugs and even a few hookers? What man in his right mind would want to be connected with a crowd like that, let alone eat dinner with them?

But that's exactly what Jesus wanted to do—and exactly what he did. When Jesus said, "Healthy people don't need a doctor," he was in essence saying that Matthew and his mixed-up friends did need a doctor. They were despised by their neighbors, their lives were going sideways, and they were probably miserable. And yet they welcomed Jesus into their homes—and eventually into their hearts. They were eager to receive forgiveness and healing—they were ready for a fresh start.

My Prayer

Dear God,
Help me to realize how much I need you. I want to welcome you into my heart and into my life the same way Matthew did. Thank you for forgiving me!
Amen.

Stone
for the Journey

When we admit our neediness, we are ready to receive help.

Final Word

But the tax collector stood at a distance and dared not even lift his eyes to heaven as he prayed. Instead, he beat his chest in sorrow, saying, "O God, be merciful to me, for I am a sinner."

Luke 18:13 NLT

60

Religious Acts

One day some followers of John the Baptist came and asked Jesus, "Why do we and the Pharisees often go without eating, while your disciples never do?" Jesus answered: The friends of a bridegroom don't go without eating while he is still with them. But the time will come when he will be taken from them. Then they will go without eating.

Matthew 9:14–15 CEV

Our modern American culture sometimes has difficulty understanding cultures that are bound up in religious rules and traditions. It's like another world. But that was the world Jesus entered when he came to earth. And it was that world Jesus wanted to transform. Still, it wasn't easy to break through thousands of years of religion.

The ultimate goal behind all the religious rules and laws and dogma was supposedly for people to get connected to God. Unfortunately, that wasn't working. If anything, people were farther away from God than ever. That's why Jesus came—to show everyone that there was a better way to connect to God. But they still weren't getting it. Some people, even those who were trying to follow Jesus, were still caught up in the trappings of religion. For instance, fasting (going without food) seemed like an impressive religious act, and one that was sure to get attention. Why didn't Jesus fast too?

What Jesus was trying to tell and show the people was that they didn't need to fast to connect with God. God was right there with them, in the form of Jesus! Couldn't they see it? Couldn't they feel it? They'd witnessed miracles. They'd heard teaching. And yet they were still stuck in the thinking that it was up to them to connect to God.

Sometimes we do the same thing. We go through steps that we think look good. We do religious acts that are meant to impress. And yet what we fail to see is that God is right there with us! All we need to do is take Jesus's hand—and we're connected to God.

My Prayer

Dear God,
I don't want to put on a religious act for you. I don't want to try to impress anyone. Help me to remember that you are right here with me. Help me to stay connected.
Amen.

Final Word

> In certain ways we are weak, but the Spirit is here to help us. For example, when we don't know what to pray for, the Spirit prays for us in ways that cannot be put into words.
>
> Romans 8:26 CEV

Stone
for the Journey

God wants us not to jump through hoops but to bring our open hearts to him.

61

Transformed Thinking

Besides, who would patch old clothing with new cloth? For the new patch would shrink and rip away from the old cloth, leaving an even bigger tear than before.

And no one puts new wine into old wineskins. For the old skins would burst from the pressure, spilling the wine and ruining the skins. New wine is stored in new wineskins so that both are preserved.

Matthew 9:16–17 NLT

Jesus is speaking in metaphors again—using parables to make a point. But what is he really saying? First of all, he makes this statement right after he tells his followers that they don't need to do a "religious" act to connect to God—because God is right there among them in the form of Jesus! But he wants to drive this point home further by speaking their language. Unfortunately, it's not really our language or the language of modern culture.

What Jesus is saying is that he's got something fresh and new, and it will be useless if it's stored in an old container. To put this into modern-day words, imagine that all you have is this really old computer (from the previous century), and you're trying to download a brand-new, state-of-the-art, totally cool video game on it. No matter how much you want to play that video game, it ain't gonna work. You need a new computer.

That's what Jesus is saying. You can't use your old rules and ways of practicing religion and try to fit Jesus into them. It's like trying to download a new song from the Internet onto your grandma's old stereo. No way, José.

So what does this mean to you personally? Is it possible you have some old ways of thinking? Some myths that you've adhered to? Perhaps you've created some distorted religious traditions of your own. Maybe you're superstitious about something. Let Jesus transform you (make you new) in order to fill you with himself. Come to him and say, "Okay, do what you want with me." And then let him do it.

My Prayer

Dear God,
I don't want to be like an old computer—unable to contain the latest and greatest thing that you want to do in me. Help me to change. Make me new.
Amen.

Stone
for the Journey

Change is good—when God is the one in charge of it.

Final Word

"For I know the plans I have for you," says the LORD. "They are plans for good and not for disaster, to give you a future and a hope."

Jeremiah 29:11 NLT

62

Desperate Faith

Words from the Rock

> *Just then a woman who had hemorrhaged for twelve years slipped in from behind and lightly touched his robe. She was thinking to herself, "If I can just put a finger on his robe, I'll get well." Jesus turned—caught her at it. Then he reassured her: "Courage, daughter. You took a risk of faith, and now you're well." The woman was well from then on.*
>
> Matthew 9:20–22 Message

It's hard to imagine what it would've been like to have a serious illness two thousand years ago. And without modern medicine or modern conveniences, even something like a common cold could be miserable. So it's easy to understand how people were drawn to Jesus simply because of his power to heal. Without good doctors, medication, or hospitals, they were desperate for miracles.

And the woman who had suffered from hemorrhaging for twelve years must've been truly miserable. To complicate matters, in her culture a woman was considered "unclean" while having her period, and, as a result, she had all kinds of rules to follow—as well as having a stigma attached—until she was "clean" again. And this poor woman hadn't stopped bleeding for years. Her condition (probably a result of tumors, cysts, or even cancer) wasn't only hurting her physically, but it had to be hard on her everyday life as well. It's no wonder she snuck up behind Jesus—she probably didn't want anyone to know that an "unclean" woman was in the crowd. But Jesus knew.

Can you imagine her surprise when he turned and smiled at her? And then he told her that she'd been brave to come, and that her step of faith had made her well. In other words, there's nothing wrong with desperate faith. Jesus loves it when we come to him needing and expecting his help. He wants us to be like that desperate woman, reaching out to touch him and hoping for a miracle.

My Prayer

Dear God,
Help me to take risks with my faith—and teach me to come to you with all my problems and concerns and with the high expectation that you will help me.
Amen.

Final Word

> *And he said to her, "Daughter, your faith has made you well. Go in peace. Your suffering is over."*
>
> Mark 5:34 NLT

Stone
for the Journey

Risks are not so risky when your faith is in God and he's the one leading you.

63

Faith's Reward

Words from the Rock

> *When he had gone indoors, the blind men came to him, and he asked them, "Do you believe that I am able to do this?"*
>
> *"Yes, Lord," they replied.*
>
> *Then he touched their eyes and said, "According to your faith will it be done to you."*

Matthew 9:28–29 NIV

*D*o you ever wonder why Jesus didn't just lift up his arms and do one great big mega miracle that healed everyone all at the same time? He certainly had the power. And that sure would've saved a lot of time, not to mention travel (mostly by foot). And yet he didn't want to do it like that. He had another plan.

Jesus knew there was much more at stake in his ministry than simply making people well again. He knew that health alone was not enough. He also knew that when he touched and healed people on a one-on-one basis, he entered into a partnership with them. A partnership that required something from them as well. For starters, the sick person (or their loved one) was usually the one who asked Jesus for help. That meant the person in need of healing was forced to make an effort to step out of their comfort zone, come before Jesus, admit to a problem, and then humbly ask for assistance. In other words, they were putting their trust and their lives in his hands. He had the power, and they had the need. A partnership was formed.

And when Jesus healed them, it was like the partnership was sealed. Oh, maybe that person didn't totally get it right in the moment. For sure, there must've been people who were so overjoyed with their ability to walk, see, or hear that they may have temporarily forgotten how it happened. But later on, they had to appreciate what had taken place. They must've valued the gift they'd been given. And, as a result, wouldn't they have become followers? Wouldn't they have taken that partnership to a new level of relationship by committing the rest of their lives to Jesus? Because that was his goal.

And that's still his goal with us today. He wants us to take that step of faith toward him, and then he will partner with us.

My Prayer

Dear God,
Maybe I'm not physically blind, but sometimes I'm blind in other ways. Help me to have enough faith to come to you and ask for healing. Then remind me that we are partners in this—my faith combined with your power means nothing is impossible.
Amen.

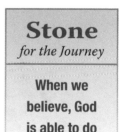

Stone
for the Journey

When we believe, God is able to do anything.

Final Word

> *Faith makes us sure of what we hope for and gives us proof of what we cannot see.*
>
> Hebrews 11:1 CEV

64

Get Ready

Words from the Rock

> *The harvest is great, but the workers are few. So*
> *pray to the Lord who is in charge of the harvest;*
> *ask him to send more workers into his fields.*
>
> Matthew 9:37–38 NLT

Jesus's earthly ministry (less than four years) was relatively short. Think about it. Most people spend more time than that in college. Yet Jesus was trying to give the world a much larger education than any four-year degree could. And as his ministry increased and the word spread as to who he was and what he could do, the crowds and their needs grew to an overwhelming number. Okay, Jesus probably wasn't a bit overwhelmed. He was God. He could handle it. But he knew that he wasn't going to be around long enough to take care of all those people himself.

There was a need for that partnership thing again. Only this time he wanted people to partner with him on an even higher level. He wanted them to help spread the Good News (forgiveness, salvation, and a relationship with God) to everyone who was waiting to hear about it. And there were a lot of people waiting—in fact, it seemed there were more people ready and waiting to hear it than there were people ready to go out and share it. That's the meaning behind his words, "The harvest is great, but the workers are few."

So what did Jesus do? He didn't tell the people to go out and gather the harvest. Instead, he told them to *pray about it*. He told them to ask God (the one in charge of the harvest) to send people out to gather his harvest and to do his work. And again, that's our invitation to partner with him. Are we praying about this? Do we remember to ask God to send missionaries to places like Sudan or India, or even around the corner? Because there's still a "harvest" out there. What will you do about it?

My Prayer

Dear God,
Show me specific ways that I can be praying for those who are still waiting to hear about you. Remind me to pray for people to go out and collect the harvest.
Amen.

Final Word

> *Don't act like them. If you want to be great, you must be the servant of all the others. And if you want to be first, you must be the slave of the rest.*
>
> Matthew 20:26–27 CEV

Stone *for the Journey*

Though many need to hear, few are willing to go, so pray that God sends more.

65

Start Here

Words from the Rock

> *Don't begin by traveling to some far-off place to convert unbelievers. And don't try to be dramatic by tackling some public enemy. Go to the lost, confused people right here in the neighborhood. Tell them that the kingdom is here. Bring health to the sick. Raise the dead. Touch the untouchables. Kick out the demons. You have been treated generously, so live generously.*
>
> Matthew 10:5–8 Message

Jesus knew that when he challenged his followers to pray for God to send out people to gather his harvest, their own hearts would be changed. Meaning that it's hard to pray for something and not become open to the possibility that God could be asking you to be part of the answer.

As a result, Jesus's disciples and other followers were suddenly willing to go out and spread the Good News themselves. And, in case you've forgotten, they lived in an era of no TV, radio, Internet, or telephone—consequently, the only way to let people know what was going on was through word of mouth. And that meant some traveling (by foot), which required time and energy. No easy task.

But they were up for the challenge. And they were ready to head off in every direction. Imagine them poring over maps, making plans, getting excited, packing their bags, resoling their sandals.

But Jesus said, "Wait." He told them to share this Good News with their own family and friends first and to start this thing right where they lived—in their own towns and neighborhoods. Because Jesus knew that those "nearby" people were just as lost and confused as those who lived hundreds of miles away. He also knew that people are sometimes more willing to listen to someone if they already have a relationship with that person. For instance, if a stranger comes to you and says, "Hey, you should buy this new CD," you might be skeptical. But if a trusted friend says the same thing, you'd probably get the CD. And Jesus says it's similar with us—before we pack our bags to go help people in Nepal, we should reach out to those around us first.

My Prayer

Dear God,
I want to be willing to share your Good News. But I know I need your help. If you really want me to start with people I know, please lead the way. Show me who and how—and give me the courage to share.
Amen.

Stone
for the Journey

Before you can love the whole world, you need to love your neighbor.

Final Word

Do not withhold good from those who deserve it when it's in your power to help them.

Proverbs 3:27 NLT

66

Keep It Simple

> *Don't think you have to put on a fund-raising*
> *campaign before you start. You don't need a lot*
> *of equipment. You are the equipment, and all*
> *you need to keep that going is three meals a day.*
> *Travel light.*
>
> Matthew 10:9–10 Message

*J*esus was still talking to his followers in this verse, giving them some tips for the adventures they were about to begin—whether it meant returning to their hometowns or returning to someplace else. And it makes sense that some of them would be concerned about all the various details involved. Because many of them had given up jobs—they lived with Jesus and trusted him for their provision while they were on the road—they suddenly got a little worried about how things would go when they stepped out on their own without Jesus. How would they fund their traveling expenses? Where would they stay? What would they eat? What did they need to take with them?

But Jesus was very casual about the whole thing. He told them not to fuss about money or what they thought they might need because he knew they already had what they needed. They'd been listening to Jesus teach and preach for some time now, and they'd seen him do miracles. The most important part of their mission was right with them, hidden safely in their hearts. Jesus had already seen to that. And he had been trying to teach them by example that God would provide them with food and take care of their basic needs. They just needed to have faith—and to go.

That's the most important thing for us to keep in mind too. When God sends us to tell someone something, he will give us what we need to do it. That means we don't need to have a Bible in hand. We don't need a little booklet or bracelet or button to give the person. We just need to have a ready and willing heart—and trust God to do the rest.

My Prayer

Dear God,
Thank you for teaching me so many good things. Thank you for changing me from the inside. And I know that if you want me to tell someone about what you're doing, you will give me what it takes to do it.
Amen.

Stone
for the Journey

God will not send you where he hasn't already equipped you to go.

Final Word

And this same God who takes care of me will supply all your needs from his glorious riches, which have been given to us in Christ Jesus.

Philippians 4:19 NLT

Reaching Out

Words from the Rock

> When you enter a town or village, don't insist on
> staying in a luxury inn. Get a modest place with
> some modest people, and be content there until
> you leave.
>
> When you knock on a door, be courteous in your
> greeting. If they welcome you, be gentle in your
> conversation. If they don't welcome you, quietly
> withdraw. Don't make a scene. Shrug your shoul-
> ders and be on your way. You can be sure that on
> Judgment Day they'll be mighty sorry—but it's no
> concern of yours now.
>
> Matthew 10:11–15 Message

*J*esus was giving even more instructions for this new
outreach ministry. But the counsel he gave his disciples
and followers then is no different than what he would say today. For
starters, Jesus points out that you don't have to seek out the best or
the fanciest accommodations. That's because he doesn't want you to
put yourself in places where you'll appear superior to the ones he's
called you to reach out to. He doesn't want you to be out of touch
with those who are in serious need.

Then he encourages you to be courteous as you speak to people. Now, that doesn't seem like a big deal, except that almost everyone has heard stories of "Christians" who attempt to "minister" in bossy, know-it-all, smug ways. And what does that accomplish? Jesus says to be thoughtful and kind, and if the person you're speaking with responds and asks you to, say, have a cup of coffee, don't turn them down. As you talk, be compassionate in your words. Instead of pointing out that person's problems, show how Jesus is loving and merciful. And then see what happens. Most people will warm up and want to hear more.

But if the person gets mad or doesn't want to listen or attempts to engage you in some ridiculous religious argument, don't make a scene. Just smile and shrug your shoulders and head on your way. It's not your fault that they don't get it. Besides, it might just be a matter of timing with that person—they might not be ready to hear the truth. But maybe you've planted some seeds of truth in them. And by you not reacting or getting mad, those seeds have a greater chance of growing someday. Remember that God is in charge of the outcome of the harvest. You're more like a tool in his hand.

My Prayer

Dear God,
There's so much to learn about telling others about you. Please teach me and show me so I can do my part.
Amen.

Final Word

Peace and prosperity to you, your family, and everything you own!

1 Samuel 25:6 NLT

Stone
for the Journey

Even the toughest customer finds it hard to reject honesty, kindness, and love.

68

Watch Out!

Words from the Rock

Words from the Rock

Stay alert. This is hazardous work I'm assigning you. You're going to be like sheep running through a wolf pack, so don't call attention to yourselves. Be as cunning as a snake, inoffensive as a dove.

Matthew 10:16 Message

*J*esus was fully aware of the serious dangers his followers would face. It was a frightening time when Christians were routinely beaten, imprisoned, or even murdered as a result of their faith. Obviously this warning was extremely relevant to them. And yet Jesus's words weren't meant only for that era—there's a warning here that still applies today.

While it's unlikely you'll be locked up or executed for your beliefs, at least in America, there are plenty of pitfalls to trip you up. The tricky part is that our modern-day challenges are a lot more subtle than the challenges of the early church were. Their opposition was blatant and threatening and in-your-face deadly. Ours is sneaky and quiet—yet just as lethal in the spiritual sense. Compare an enemy with a loaded machine gun aimed directly at your head to an enemy disguised as a friend who slips arsenic into your water. Both are out to destroy.

That's why Jesus warns you to "stay alert." He wants you to keep your eyes open and be fully aware. He wants you to realize that you will have spiritual opposition and to be on guard against it. Your enemy might hit you with the temptation to cheat on a math test or to have premarital sex or to lie to your parents. These are just some of the subtle ways your spiritual integrity can be eroded so that you are separated from God and ultimately destroyed. But Jesus wants you to be smart—to comprehend what you're up against so that you don't fall into those traps. Because although Jesus is always ready to rescue you, he knows that the more times you get caught in those traps, the harder it becomes to get out.

My Prayer

Dear God,
Help me to be alert enough to see any dangers that are lurking around the corner. But at the same time, keep me from obsessing over these things, and help me focus my attention on you. Amen.

Final Word

I am glad that everyone knows how well you obey the Lord. But still, I want you to understand what is good and not have anything to do with evil.

Romans 16:19 CEV

Stone
for the Journey

Keep your spiritual eyes open, because the most destructive enemy is sneaky and quiet and tricky.

Persecution Problems

Words from the Rock

> *Don't be naive. Some people will impugn your motives, others will smear your reputation—just because you believe in me. Don't be upset when they haul you before the civil authorities. Without knowing it, they've done you—and me—a favor, given you a platform for preaching the kingdom news! And don't worry about what you'll say or how you'll say it. The right words will be there; the Spirit of your Father will supply the words.*

Matthew 10:17–20 Message

*J*esus wants you to know that situations will come up where you are put on the spot because of your faith. That's just part of being a Christian. Whether it's a friend challenging your personal convictions, a teacher questioning your beliefs, or maybe even someone who makes false accusations just to get to you, you can expect that life won't always go smoothly. In fact, if your life is going too smoothly, you might want to wonder what that means. Because it's usually the ones who are making their best effort to follow Jesus that get hit the hardest—like a spiritual smackdown.

But Jesus is saying not to be concerned when this happens to you. In fact, he takes it a step further by saying that it's a positive thing when you meet this kind of opposition, because it gives you the opportunity to speak out about what God's doing in your life. It's like that person (the one picking on you because of your faith) has just given you the stage, the spotlight is on you, and now you get to tell anyone within hearing distance that you belong to God and that he's doing some very cool things in your life. And it's likely that some observer is going to be hugely impacted by your statement.

Okay, the idea of being the center of attention might make some people nervous. Especially ones with a phobia of public speaking. (By the way, that's the number one fear in our country.) But Jesus says not to worry about what you'll say. He promises that God will give you the right words at the time you need them. All you need to do is trust him to do that. Just don't forget that it's all about him—not you.

My Prayer

Dear God,
Prepare me for times when I get smacked down because I'm living my life for you. Help me to trust you for just the right words to answer my opposition.
Amen.

Stone
for the Journey

When you live all-out for God, you should expect some opposition.

Final Word

This should prove to you that I am speaking for Christ. When he corrects you, he won't be weak. He will be powerful!

2 Corinthians 13:3 CEV

70

Hang In There

When people realize it is the living God you are presenting and not some idol that makes them feel good, they are going to turn on you, even people in your own family. There is a great irony here: proclaiming so much love, experiencing so much hate! But don't quit. Don't cave in. It is all well worth it in the end. It is not success you are after in such times but survival. Be survivors! Before you've run out of options, the Son of Man will have arrived.

Matthew 10:21–23 Message

*P*eople who aren't living for God sometimes feel threatened by those who are. For instance, if you're seen doing something that shows you have a different moral code (say, you're trying to obey God by not drinking alcohol), it might make someone (the guy who thinks it's cool to drink alcohol) feel uncomfortable. As a result, you might have to take some flak. There's also a chance that someone in your own family or maybe a friend will turn against you if you stand up for what you believe (and it's not what they believe). Jesus said to expect this.

He also said that even if you handle a tough situation in a really kind and nonjudgmental way—like you show a person you love them despite your differences—the person might still turn on you. In fact, they might return your kindness with hostility and hatred. But don't let that stop you from being loving and patient with that person, because that's how hearts are changed. At the very least, *you* will be changed. When you love someone who's picking on you, it's like you're loving with a very pure, godly love—and, as a result, you become more like him.

Jesus says even if it gets really, really hard, don't give up. Hang in there. And be assured that God will never ask more than you (with his power) are able to take. Just when it feels hopeless, he'll step in and intervene.

My Prayer

Dear God,
Help me to remember that I will be picked on because of you—and that that's a good thing. Please love others through me.
Amen.

Stone
for the Journey

Don't be surprised when God's goodness threatens nonbelievers.

Final Word

Everyone will hate you because of me. But if you keep on being faithful right to the end, you will be saved.

Mark 13:13 CEV

71

Be Bold

Words from the Rock

Don't be afraid of anyone! Everything that is hidden will be found out, and every secret will be known. Whatever I say to you in the dark, you must tell in the light. And you must announce from the housetops whatever I have whispered to you.

Matthew 10:26–27 CEV

Jesus knows it's not easy living a Christian life in a world that doesn't always get it. Even so, he wants you to have total confidence in him. He wants your faith to be so rock solid that you will reach that place where you realize you can't be frightened or intimidated by anyone. Where you accept that God is bigger and stronger—and you're assured that he's looking out for you.

Does that mean you can swagger down the halls at school like you own the place, like no one or nothing can hurt you? Probably not. And why would you even want to? Think about it. How did Jesus act when he walked the earth? In spite of the fact that he knew he was one with God, that he had all the power and authority of his Father, and that he could call down lightning bolts to wipe out all his enemies with one swift blow, he didn't. In fact, he eventually allowed himself to be beaten and ridiculed and nailed to a cross. Yet the whole while, he knew that he had far more power and authority than the ones who killed him.

It's that quiet kind of confidence that gets people's attention. It's that calm attitude of humble faith that stands out in a crowd full of boasters. It's that knowledge that you are linked to the power of the universe. Even if you look like a nobody to some people, your Father in heaven will eventually set things straight. He'll make it known that you are valuable because you belong to him.

My Prayer

Dear God,
I want a rock-solid kind of faith. Help me to get to that place where my trust in you is so strong that I'm not afraid and I know you are taking care of me.
Amen.

Stone
for the Journey

Where faith lives strong, there is no room for fear.

Final Word

Whatever you have said in the dark will be heard in the light, and what you have whispered behind closed doors will be shouted from the housetops for all to hear!

Luke 12:3 NLT

Don't Fear

72

Words from the Rock

Don't be bluffed into silence by the threats of bullies. There's nothing they can do to your soul, your core being. Save your fear for God, who holds your entire life—body and soul—in his hands.

Matthew 10:28 Message

In this verse, Jesus encourages you to take your rock-solid faith to an even deeper level. Instead of simply being free from fear, he challenges you to speak up for him while surrounded by nonbelievers. And not just those quiet, apathetic nonbelievers either. He's talking about those antagonistic kind of nonbelievers, those bully types with an ax to grind.

Okay, that sounds a little intimidating, doesn't it? Who would want to stumble into a satanic street meeting wearing a WWJD T-shirt? And, seriously, if God wasn't the one prompting you to do this, you probably shouldn't. But if you find yourself in a dicey situation and you sincerely believe God is nudging you to speak for him, you can do it with the bold confidence that he's backing you. And as Jesus has pointed out, he will give you the words. Chances are, the outcome will be amazing—even if it doesn't seem that way at the time—and you can be assured that God is up to something big.

But here's the main point of this verse: Jesus is saying not to be afraid of someone who can physically hurt or even kill you, because doing that gives that person power over you, power that really doesn't belong to them. The only one you should give that kind of power to is God—because he's the ruler of the universe and has all power and authority, and he's the one responsible for every important part of your life. In other words, you're in good hands.

My Prayer

Dear God,
Help me not to be intimidated by anyone. Let me be assured that only you have real power over me. And remind me that you only want the best for me.
Amen.

Stone
for the Journey

Humans might try to bluff through intimidation, but God holds all the cards.

Final Word

He was quite explicit: "Vengeance is mine, and I won't overlook a thing" and "God will judge his people." Nobody's getting by with anything, believe me.

Hebrews 10:30–31 Message

73

Your Value

Words from the Rock

What's the price of a pet canary? Some loose change, right? And God cares what happens to it even more than you do. He pays even greater attention to you, down to the last detail—even numbering the hairs on your head! So don't be intimidated by all this bully talk. You're worth more than a million canaries.

Matthew 10:29–31 Message

Although we need to understand and respect that God is the greatest superpower of the universe, Jesus also wants us to remember how valuable we are to him. And this isn't an easy concept to grasp, because our human way of thinking suggests that the more significant and influential a person is (like the president or a celebrity), the more likely it is that person wouldn't give us the time of day. And yet God is way more powerful and way more important than any person on the planet.

It's hard to imagine how small we are compared to God—we're like one tiny droplet, and he is the entire ocean. And yet God knows every single thing about us clear down to how many hairs are on our heads (and that number changes daily). So perhaps you wonder,

How can God be so huge and so mighty and care about someone as insignificant as me? Because he is God—it's just who he is. And it's impossible for us to wrap our earthly minds around that concept.

But Jesus is reminding us that God is intimately involved in our lives and that God loves us more than we can imagine. And for that reason we should rest assured that he will take care of us—and that he will see us through life's hardest challenges.

My Prayer

Dear God,
Help me to comprehend how powerful and amazing you are. Thank you for placing such great value in me.
Amen.

Stone
for the Journey

God knows everything about me, and yet he loves me.

Final Word

How much more valuable is a man than a sheep! Therefore it is lawful to do good on the Sabbath.

Matthew 12:12 NIV

74

Stay Strong

Words from the Rock

> *Whoever acknowledges me before men, I will also acknowledge him before my Father in heaven. But whoever disowns me before men, I will disown him before my Father in heaven.*
>
> Matthew 10:32–33 NIV

It's good to have a private relationship with God. Those intimate times when you go one-on-one with your heavenly Father help you to grow. And those quiet moments draw you closer to God as well as strengthen your faith. But if you always keep your faith private, if you keep your beliefs to yourself and your lips sealed, something is wrong.

What if you fell in love and were planning to get married, but you never told anyone about it? Maybe your fiancé asked if you wanted to put an announcement in the local paper, but you said, "No, that's too embarrassing." Would your fiancé think you were ashamed? Maybe he would question your commitment. Because most newly engaged people can't wait to tell everyone. Wouldn't keeping quiet be cause for concern?

That might be similar to how Jesus feels when you're unwilling to talk about him. He might wonder about your commitment level or think that you're ashamed to be in a relationship with him. And it would probably make him sad.

Jesus wants you to speak freely about his involvement in your life. He wants you to be open about what he's doing and what he's done for you. It's one of the main ways he draws others to himself. But if you keep your mouth shut or act like you don't know him, it's a serious concern. In fact, doing that suggests that maybe you don't really know him at all. And if that's the case, how will he know you? How will he present you to his Father?

My Prayer

Dear God,
Help me to speak freely about you to anyone who wants to hear. Show me natural ways to bring up what you're doing in my life without shoving it down someone's throat.
Amen.

> **Stone**
> *for the Journey*
>
> **I won't hide my relationship with Jesus from anyone.**

Final Word

> *And I say to you, everyone who confesses Me before men, the Son of Man will confess him also before the angels of God.*
>
> Luke 12:8 NASB

Tough Stuff

Words from the Rock

*Don't think I've come to make life cozy. I've come
to cut—make a sharp knife-cut between son and
father, daughter and mother, bride and mother-
in-law—cut through these cozy domestic arrange-
ments and free you for God. Well-meaning family
members can be your worst enemies. If you prefer
father or mother over me, you don't deserve me.
If you prefer son or daughter over me, you don't
deserve me.*

Matthew 10:34–37 Message

Again, Jesus was encouraging his disciples and followers to
brace themselves for some tough times ahead. And, for
sure, the disciples were about to enter into some pretty treacherous
territory. Jesus didn't want to deceive them, and he wasn't about to
tell them that following him would be just a walk in the park. More
like a walk through a minefield.

While your life probably won't be threatened as a result of your
faith, it's possible that you could endure some challenges that were
similar to those of the disciples. For instance, it's likely that not all
your family members will share your beliefs. In fact, there might be

some who will criticize you for your faith. They might even ridicule you or try to talk you out of it. There might be some who will cut you off or freeze you out. It could be the price you will pay for following Jesus. But does that mean you should back down? Should you set aside your faith in order to please your family? Of course not.

Jesus makes it clear that if you choose your family (even your parents) over him, you are making a serious mistake. If you allow even the most loving family member to convince you to abandon your faith, you will be sorry. And you won't be sorry only for your own sake, but you will also be sorry for theirs—when you realize that if you'd stuck to your beliefs, perhaps they would've joined you eventually. So, even if it's tough, hold firm to your faith. Trust God more than family or friends or anyone—and in the end you will not regret it.

My Prayer

Dear God,
I choose to put you first in my life. Even if my family doesn't support my faith, I will follow you. Please help them to see your work in me and to want you to be first in their lives too. Amen.

Final Word

> Do you think that I came to bring peace to earth? No indeed! I came to make people choose sides.

Luke 12:51 CEV

Total Trust

Words from the Rock

> *And unless you are willing to take up your cross and come with me, you are not fit to be my disciples. If you try to save your life, you will lose it. But if you give it up for me, you will surely find it.*
>
> Matthew 10:38–39 CEV

Some people think the image of a cross is lovely. You see artistic versions of it in churches, on walls, even around people's necks. But back when Jesus made this statement, the cross was equivalent to a hangman's noose or an electric chair. It was the symbol of death. To "take up your cross" meant being ready to die for something—or someone. It was a total commitment—no backing down, all the way.

And that's the "invitation" Jesus was offering his disciples? Death? As devoted as they were to him, it must've been fairly startling to hear those words. Imagine these guys scratching their heads and glancing nervously at each other. Was Jesus really asking them to die for him? If so, was that a price they were willing to pay? Perhaps at the time of hearing this, they weren't too sure. But before their lives ended (mostly by painful executions), Jesus's disciples would not only come to grips with this invitation, they would gladly accept it.

What does that mean for you? Is Jesus asking you to die for him too? Maybe. But more than that, he's asking you *to live for him*. He's asking you to put aside personal goals and selfish dreams and to come to him for direction. He's inviting you to trust him so completely that you're willing to put your life in his hands. Because he knows if you try to live life your way, it will only disappoint you. But the way to a real life—one that's fulfilling and rewarding and genuine—is by receiving it from him.

My Prayer

Dear God,
Help me to accept your invitation to a real life.
Show me how to set aside my ways in exchange for your ways.
Amen.

Stone
for the Journey

If I cling to my life, it will vanish, but in God's hands it will flourish.

Final Word

In the same way, anyone who holds on to life just as it is destroys that life. But if you let it go, reckless in your love, you'll have it forever, real and eternal.

John 12:25 Message

77

Welcome!

Words from the Rock

> *Anyone who welcomes you welcomes me. And anyone who welcomes me also welcomes the one who sent me.*
>
> Matthew 10:40 CEV

This straightforward Scripture is actually rather profound in its simplicity. And for a relatively short verse, it holds a whopper of a promise. Jesus says that if someone welcomes you, they are likewise welcoming him—and not only him, but his Father as well. In other words, he's saying that you're like an ambassador of salvation to the people you interact with. They welcome you . . . they welcome God. But what does that really mean?

Is Jesus saying that if you knock on a friend's door and your friend says, "Hey, welcome, come on in," that means they're saying the same thing to God? Maybe so. But does that mean your friend, who doesn't claim to be a Christian, really is one? Maybe not. Or maybe not yet. It could just be a question of timing. So perhaps the bigger question here is, how do you get someone to welcome you? What does that entail?

Think about it. What causes you to accept others? What makes you want to welcome someone into your world? What does a good friend do that encourages you to open up and talk? That's not hard to answer. It's usually because of the way you're treated. When someone shows you genuine love and respect, when they're sincere and kind and caring, you can't help but want to be around that person. And when you're like that to others, they suddenly become open to what you have to say—even if you want to tell them about what God is doing in your life.

My Prayer

Dear God,
Help me to be the kind of person that people welcome into their lives. Let my words and actions be motivated by love so that my friends will see you in me.
Amen.

Final Word

> *In a loud voice Jesus said: Everyone who has faith in me also has faith in the one who sent me.*

John 12:44 CEV

Stone
for the Journey

When I'm caring, loving, and kind, I show that God is caring, loving, and kind.

78

Team Effort

> *Accepting a messenger of God is as good as being God's messenger. Accepting someone's help is as good as giving someone help. This is a large work I've called you into, but don't be overwhelmed by it.*
>
> Matthew 10:41 Message

God made you unique—as a result, he doesn't expect you to live the same life or do the same things as someone else. And although the previous few verses focused on spreading the good news about connecting others to God, not everyone has the same abilities and gifts to get the job done. Fortunately, God doesn't want everyone to be an evangelist or a missionary—and the world would be a crazy place if everyone wanted to be a preacher or teacher or leader. It really takes all kinds.

That's why God chose something special for each of us to do, a distinct way we can each do our part to assist in his big plans. And being that God is God and infinitely creative, he's created you with specific gifts, gifts that he wants you to put to good use. Maybe it's the gift of being a loyal friend. Maybe you're good at listening. Maybe you like to help people. Maybe you're a good encourager. Those are all gifts—and all are useful as long as we're using them to help each other. God wants us to learn how to be team players. He wants us to cooperate with each other, to value our individual gifts, and to be willing to put them to good use.

So if you have a friend who's really good at sharing his faith, you might be gifted at encouraging him. Or maybe you have a friend with a knack for teaching from the Bible, but she's not very organized, so you help to keep her on track. Even when you're behind the scenes, what you are doing is valuable. Jesus said it is equally as valuable as what the person out in front is doing. So whatever it is, do your part!

My Prayer

Dear God,
Help me to recognize what my gifts are—and then to use them. I want to be a committed team player, helping my teammates, with you as the captain.
Amen.

Final Word

By this we know that we love the children of God, when we love God and observe His commandments.

1 John 5:2 NASB

Stone
for the Journey

When we appreciate our individual gifts and work as a team, God gets the glory.

Acts of Kindness

> *And anyone who gives one of my most humble followers a cup of cool water, just because that person is my follower, will surely be rewarded.*
>
> Matthew 10:42 CEV

Getting someone a drink of water doesn't seem like a big deal, but Jesus said that if someone does something that seemingly insignificant for one of his followers, that person will be rewarded.

This suggests two things. For starters, Jesus is making a statement about how devoted he is to his followers. He's saying that they are so valued to him, so important, so dearly loved, that it gets his attention whenever someone treats them with kindness. Jesus is also saying he cares deeply about the person who shows kindness. And he doesn't say that the person has to be a believer either. He simply states that he will reward the person who shows kindness.

But here are some questions for you: What if you're serving Jesus and a nonbeliever offers to do something kind for you—and you reject their kindness? What if you just shrug and say, "No thanks, I don't need your help"? Does that rob that person of a reward? According to this verse, that could be the case. So think about it. The next time someone tries to help you or does something for you or shows you some kindness, why not accept it and say thank you—and know that by doing so, you are helping that person to be rewarded. Perhaps the real reward is that a relationship has begun—which hopefully, in time, will help that person to discover God loves him or her just as much as he loves you.

My Prayer

Dear God,
Help me to be a good receiver. Don't let my pride get in the way if a person offers help. Remind me that you want to reward that person through me.
Amen.

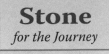

Stone
for the Journey

When I accept
help from
nonbelievers,
I allow them
to be blessed.

Final Word

For whoever gives you a cup of water to drink because of your name as followers of Christ, truly I say to you, he will not lose his reward.

Mark 9:41 NASB

Miracles

Words from the Rock

Go back and tell . . .

The blind see,
The lame walk,
Lepers are cleansed,
The deaf hear,
The dead are raised,
The wretched of the earth learn that God is on
their side.

Is this what you were expecting? Then count your-
selves most blessed!

Matthew 11:4–6 Message

*P*robably the most amazing, mind-blowing, and crowd-gathering part of Jesus's short but intense ministry was when he performed miracles. And why not? After all, he was God's Son, and he wanted to get the world's attention. What better way to get people to sit up and take notice? But that wasn't his only reason for doing miracles. Otherwise he could've done wonders like parting the Sea of Galilee. He could've made mountains walk or pigs fly. But Jesus chose to do *personal* miracles. He touched people with his own two hands, reaching right down to where people lived—and then he made them whole.

That's because Jesus had enormous compassion for the people he'd come to help—and especially those who were in great need. Rather than wanting to impress or entertain them, he wanted to change their lives. And, naturally, the word got around that something was going on. But think about it. What if you had been blind and Jesus touched you, and you could suddenly see? What would you do? Well, you'd probably run around and see everything you'd been missing, but you'd also tell people. And so Jesus's plan worked. He performed personal miracles for people, and they performed word-of-mouth advertising for him.

In many ways, it's not much different today. Jesus comes into your life. He does something amazing, and you want to tell others about it. Okay, maybe he doesn't raise you from the dead literally, but maybe he gives you a life unlike anything you've had before. That's something to talk about!

My Prayer

Dear God,
Thank you for being personal in my life. Just knowing you is a miracle. Show me new ways to tell others about what you're doing in me.
Amen.

Final Word

> *The blind will see,*
> *and the ears of the deaf*
> *will be healed.*
>
> Isaiah 35:5 CEV

Stone
for the Journey

God's miracles in my life can have a big impact on those around me.

81

Can You Hear Me Now?

Words from the Rock

Are you listening to me? Really listening?

Matthew 11:15 Message

If you have ears, pay attention!

Matthew 11:15 CEV

He who has ears, let him hear.

Matthew 11:15 NIV

Have you ever considered what a distractingly noisy world you live in? And not just when you're out doing things, but even when you're alone. Whether it's from a cell phone, an iPod, a TV, websites, video games, or whatever, some people never really experience a real sense of silence. In fact, some people get extremely uncomfortable when it gets too quiet. Have you ever noticed how some people walk into a room and immediately turn on the TV or radio or CD player? Maybe you're one of those people.

Jesus is asking, "Can you hear me now? Are you even listening? Do you know how to tune in to my voice?" If the volume of everything else in your life is turned up full blast, how can you possibly hear God speaking to you? How can you even hear yourself? And what happens when you turn the volume down? Are your ears still ringing? Have your ears grown hard of hearing because of the constant chatter that's usually going on? Maybe you just need to give yourself some quiet time—turn off everything around you and practice the art of just listening. See if you can learn how to really hear.

God's voice is described as a gentle whisper . . . so quiet that you won't hear it unless you're really focused. So quiet that you won't hear it if there's noise all around you—or if there's noise inside you. So give yourself some time to learn how to listen. Allow yourself the privilege of experiencing the rare commodity of golden silence. And see if God doesn't speak to you.

My Prayer

Dear God,
Show me the value of being quiet. Help me to get comfortable without constant noise. Teach me to tune in to you and really listen.
Amen.

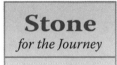

Stone
for the Journey

When my world is too noisy, it's difficult to hear God.

Final Word

If you have ears, listen to what the Spirit says to the churches. I will let everyone who wins the victory eat from the life-giving tree in God's wonderful garden.

Revelation 2:7 CEV

82

Spoiled Children

Words from the Rock

> *How can I account for this generation? The people have been like spoiled children whining to their parents, "We wanted to skip rope, and you were always too tired; we wanted to talk, but you were always too busy." John came fasting and they called him crazy. I came feasting and they called me a lush, a friend of the riffraff. Opinion polls don't count for much, do they? The proof of the pudding is in the eating.*
>
> Matthew 11:16–19 Message

ost of us don't really seem to know what we want. Oh, we might know what we want to eat for lunch or recognize some other immediate need, but when it comes to the larger picture, many of us aren't too sure. Maybe it's because we don't take the time to really think about our lives and where they're headed. Or maybe we're just generally distracted.

But Jesus came to earth with a very specific plan. A plan that a lot of people just didn't get—at least while he was in their midst. Later on, after Jesus was no longer with them, they began to grasp what he had been up to. Through the help of the Holy Spirit, people finally understood that Jesus's plan had been to connect himself with people—all people—and to reunite them to God. It was actually fairly simple.

And it's just that simple today. Jesus's plan hasn't changed a bit. He still wants to connect with us and reunite us to God. But some people refuse to accept this. They want it their way. They want to play "religious" games that confuse and complicate things so that Jesus's plan starts to look murky and eventually gets lost by the wayside. Jesus compares those people to spoiled children—because they want everything *their* way. It's as if they are determined not to figure out that God has a better way. And so they don't. But Jesus wants us to focus on him, to separate his way from all the games and distractions that might try to trip us. And then we won't be like spoiled children, whining because they didn't get their own way.

My Prayer

Dear God,
Don't let me be like a spoiled kid, throwing a tantrum because things aren't going my way. Help me to understand that your way is best. I want your way for my life.
Amen.

Final Word

> So you have not received a spirit that makes you fearful slaves. Instead, you received God's Spirit when he adopted you as his own children. Now we call him, "Abba, Father."
>
> Romans 8:15 NLT

Stone
for the Journey

When I demand my own way, I end up lost . . . but God's way leads me back.

83

God's Ways

> *Abruptly Jesus broke into prayer: "Thank you, Father, Lord of heaven and earth. You've concealed your ways from sophisticates and know-it-alls, but spelled them out clearly to ordinary people. Yes, Father, that's the way you like to work."*
>
> Matthew 11:25–26 Message

The wiser you get, the more you know how little you know. Okay, maybe that sounds confusing, but it's true. People who think they know everything usually have closed minds and consequently never learn anything new. It's like they live in a little metal box that nothing can penetrate. But people who admit they don't know it all are open to learning and will naturally become wiser. Those people are like sponges, able to soak up knowledge like water.

Jesus's prayer in these verses was related to the reception he'd received from "impressive" cities where he'd ministered and done miracles. Places where the religious, educated people had rejected him and refused to believe he'd been sent by God. In comparison, Jesus did similar miracles in some of the more rural and "less sophisticated" regions, and that's where people listened and got excited.

These ordinary people were open to Jesus. They wanted to learn new things, and they were ready to receive.

But not much has changed more than two thousand years later. When you think you know all there is to know (which is impossible), you allow pride to take over, and you shut yourself down. On the other hand, if you admit and accept that you'll never know all there is to know, and if you're eager to experience more of Jesus, you open yourself up for all he has for you. You put yourself in a position to grow and learn to become the best you can possibly be.

My Prayer

Dear God,
Please help me to remember that I'll never know it all. Keep my heart humble and eager to learn more from you.
Amen.

Final Word

With praises from children
and from tiny infants,
you have built a fortress.
It makes your enemies silent,
and all who turn against you
are left speechless.

Psalm 8:2 CEV

Stone
for the Journey

When I assume I have all the answers, I forget where to go with my questions.

84

Knowing God

Words from the Rock

> *My Father has given me everything, and he is the only one who knows the Son. The only one who truly knows the Father is the Son. But the Son wants to tell others about the Father, so that they can know him too.*
>
> Matthew 11:27 CEV

As you've heard, the primary goal of Jesus's ministry was to connect people to God. Plain and simple. And yet it was never easy. Not because Jesus wasn't equipped for the task, since he obviously had all the power and authority. It was difficult because so many people didn't want to listen. They were so entrenched in their old religion and binding laws and confining traditions that it became a huge challenge for Jesus to break through to them. It's like their culture was a huge obstacle.

Unfortunately, that can still happen today. The culture can be a barrier between you and God. Maybe it's not old religious laws that hold you back. But perhaps you have some contemporary obstacle that stands between you and knowing God. It could be a way of thinking, some activity, or an ideal—something that builds a big wall between you and God. Maybe you even know exactly what it is.

In the same way that Jesus wanted to break through those barriers during his earthly ministry so long ago, he wants to break through them with you today. Because he knows God and God knows him, he wants to knock down any walls that would keep you outside of that inner circle. He wants to connect you to himself and, as a result, connect you to God.

My Prayer

Dear God,
Show me what stands as a barrier between
me and you. Then help me to knock it down. I
don't want anything to separate me from you
and your love.
Amen.

Stone
for the Journey

**When I know
Jesus, I
know God.**

Final Word

*You gave him [Jesus] power over all people, so that
he would give eternal life to everyone you give him.
Eternal life is to know you, the only true God, and
to know Jesus Christ, the one you sent.*

John 17:2–3 CEV

85

Real Rest

Words from the Rock

Are you tired? Worn out? Burned out on religion? Come to me. Get away with me and you'll recover your life. I'll show you how to take a real rest. Walk with me and work with me—watch how I do it. Learn the unforced rhythms of grace. I won't lay anything heavy or ill-fitting on you. Keep company with me and you'll learn to live freely and lightly.

Matthew 11:28–30 Message

*R*eligion can really wear a person out. Back when Jesus was ministering, there were a lot of people who felt totally burned out by it. They were weary from jumping through all the religious hoops. They were sick and tired of feeling guilty for being unable to obey all the tedious and often ridiculous laws, and they were fed up with being fined when they didn't. Yet, when Jesus offered them a break from it all, they were hesitant to accept. And maybe understandably so.

Because they were accustomed to such religious bondage, they were probably worried that they'd be in big trouble if they "strayed" from the religious norm and followed Jesus. They knew that local religious leaders and family members could ostracize them for doing something so *radical*. And yet eventually many did. And when they followed Jesus, it was like a breath of fresh air. It was like taking off a scratchy woolen jacket on a warm summer day. Or removing a backpack loaded with bricks and leaving it behind.

Jesus offers the same thing to us. He invites us to set down the heavy loads we sometimes carry—whether someone has laid them on us or we just happened to pick them up. Jesus wants us to be unencumbered and to live in a place of rest with him. Does that mean we'll just sit around and do nothing? Of course not. But what he invites us to do won't beat us down and wear us out. Instead it will energize and invigorate us.

My Prayer

> Dear God,
> I do want to give my heavy load to you. I want to learn how to walk with you without being weighed down. Please show me how.
> Amen.

Stone
for the Journey

Jesus won't load me down with useless baggage.

Final Word

> *Those who feel tired and worn out will find new life and energy, and when they sleep, they will wake up refreshed.*
>
> Jeremiah 31:25–26 CEV

Religion versus Relationship

86

Words from the Rock

I tell you that there is something here greater than the temple. Don't you know what the Scriptures mean when they say, "Instead of offering sacrifices to me, I want you to be merciful to others?" If you knew what this means, you would not condemn these innocent disciples of mine. So the Son of Man is Lord over the Sabbath.

Matthew 12:6–8 CEV

Jesus really was a radical. Almost everything he said and did upset the local Jewish leaders. But it was about time someone rocked their world. And Jesus was the only one who could do it. At first the pompous leaders merely tolerated Jesus as a fanatic who would eventually fade away. But as his popularity grew, they made attempts to trip him up, hoping he'd fall on his face. As a result, it was the arrogant religious leaders themselves who wound up looking silly.

And when these leaders questioned the disciples' respect for the Sabbath, Jesus came back with a challenge straight from their

Scriptures. He reminded them that God would rather have merciful hearts than sacrifices. Then he pointed out that they didn't even understand what that meant.

Not only did Jesus understand what that Scripture meant, he lived it out right before their very eyes. He publicly displayed kindness and mercy and forgiveness by reaching out to anyone and everyone. He showed them, through his actions, how God wanted them all to live. Not with the same old stodgy focus on religion and rules, but with a fresh commitment to love each other and to show mercy. Now that was radical!

And that's what Jesus wants from you. He wants you to imitate him by loving and forgiving others, by building relationships instead of playing at religion.

My Prayer

Dear God,
I don't want to be religious. Help me to
be like you—to love and forgive and build
relationships.
Amen.

Stone
for the Journey

**Religion
ties your
hands, but
relationship
opens them.**

Final Word

> *I'd rather for you to be faithful*
> *and to know me*
> *than to offer sacrifices.*
>
> Hosea 6:6 CEV

87

Law versus Life

Words from the Rock

> He replied, "Is there a person here who, finding one of your lambs fallen into a ravine, wouldn't, even though it was a Sabbath, pull it out? Surely kindness to people is as legal as kindness to animals!" Then he said to the man, "Hold out your hand." He held it out and it was healed. The Pharisees walked out furious, sputtering about how they were going to ruin Jesus.
>
> Matthew 12:11–14 Message

Once again, the Pharisees were challenging Jesus. They told him it was unlawful to heal on the Sabbath. The original law was to respect the Sabbath as a day of rest and to keep it holy. But over the years, there had been hundreds of restrictive legal addenda to that law, stating things like how far people were allowed to travel (not far) or what they were allowed to carry (not much). There were even laws for what people were allowed to rescue from their homes if they caught on fire.

So once again, Jesus responded, reminding them of some of their own addenda to the Sabbath law. For instance, you weren't allowed to lift anything heavy on the Sabbath, but if your lamb fell into a ravine, it was okay to get it out. So Jesus applied this to people, saying that if they could be kind to an animal, why was it wrong to be kind to a human? And when he healed the man on the Sabbath, the Pharisees were enraged—they accused him of breaking the law.

Jesus's point was to show that God was more concerned with loving and helping people than with keeping the Pharisees' crazy rules and regulations. It was a point he made over and over again. Unfortunately, the most religious people rarely got it. They didn't even want to get it. They were too caught up in their own world.

But we can get caught up in our own world too. We can become so self-focused that we don't see where Jesus is trying to lead us. So before we find ourselves in a corner, let's open our eyes and our ears—tune in to him.

My Prayer

Dear God,
Thanks for reminding me, again, that you care more about people and relationships than anything. Help me to keep my eyes on you. Amen.

Stone *for the Journey*

God's love in me results in acts of kindness toward others.

Final Word

I am not trying to please people. I want to please God. Do you think I am trying to please people? If I were doing that, I would not be a servant of Christ.

Galatians 1:10 CEV

88

Real Power

Words from the Rock

*But if I am casting out demons by the Spirit of God,
then the Kingdom of God has arrived among you.
For who is powerful enough to enter the house of
a strong man like Satan and plunder his goods?
Only someone even stronger—someone who could
tie him up and then plunder his house.*

Matthew 12:28–29 NLT

The Pharisees were at it again. This time they accused Jesus of being connected to Satan, saying, "How else could he do his magic tricks?" They honestly believed Jesus got his power from Satan! It might have been laughable except that it was so mean-spirited on their part. Naturally, Jesus came back with a great response, asking why he would cast out demons (Satan's little friends) if he was in partnership with Satan. Wouldn't that be slightly self-defeating?

But the Pharisees were searching for something—anything—to discredit Jesus's power and authority. And the more they tried, the sillier they looked. Still, it's cool to see how Jesus took advantage of their attacks. He used their accusations to teach bystanders, to make important points, and to gently but firmly expose the Pharisees' ignorant arrogance. And the whole while he had enough power to annihilate them all. But he didn't. That's real power—power under control, power that makes the most out of a tough situation.

God wants to do the same thing in your life today. What tough situation are you facing? What challenge feels insurmountable to you? Give it to God. Trust his power to transform pain or suffering into something good. Because God won't waste anything when you let him in.

My Prayer

Dear God,
Thank you for being the most powerful force in the universe. And thank you for caring for me. Use your power to change my world.
Amen.

Final Word

God's children cannot keep on being sinful. His life-giving power lives in them and makes them his children, so that they cannot keep on sinning.

1 John 3:9 CEV

Stone
for the Journey

My hardships are transformed into strengths with God's power.

89

Cling to the Holy Spirit

Words from the Rock

> *I tell you that any sinful thing you do or say can be forgiven. Even if you speak against the Son of Man, you can be forgiven. But if you speak against the Holy Spirit, you can never be forgiven, either in this life or in the life to come.*
>
> Matthew 12:31–32 CEV

Because of this Scripture, some Christians worry that it's possible to lose their salvation and be unforgivable. But that's certainly not Jesus's plan. He's just warning us to be careful. He's saying, don't slam or slander God's Holy Spirit. But what does that really mean? Is he suggesting that if we get angry and say something stupid against the Holy Spirit that we will be struck down with lightning and go to hell? Probably not. But he is strongly cautioning us—he wants us to understand how serious our words are.

There are a series of steps—rather, missteps—that are possible for you to take, and if you do, you could arrive at the place that's "unforgivable." For starters, you could decide to disobey God, resulting in some form of sin in your life. Jesus says that he's still there and ready to forgive you. But what if you don't come to him? What if you refuse to confess your sin, and you refuse to be forgiven? And what if that makes you bitter, and, as a result, you get mad at Jesus? Well, Jesus says he can still forgive you for that—you just need to come to him and ask.

But what if you don't? What if you allow your heart to become so hard and bitter that you say bad things about the Holy Spirit? Remember, the Holy Spirit is the quiet God-voice inside you—the personal link who connects you to God. What happens when you tell the Holy Spirit to take a hike? It's possible that at that point you've reached a place where you've turned your back on God. You've shoved him out of your life and severed all ties. And that means you no longer have a relationship with him—period. Jesus says don't go there.

My Prayer

Dear God,
Please help me to confess any and all sins to you ASAP. Help me to keep a clean slate and to never become bitter toward you.
Amen.

Final Word

> *God has shown us how kind he is by coming to save all people. He taught us to give up our wicked ways and our worldly desires and to live decent and honest lives in this world.*
>
> Titus 2:11–12 CEV

Stone
for the Journey

God won't turn his back on me unless I turn my back on him first.

90

The Power of Words

Words from the Rock

> *A good tree produces only good fruit, and a bad tree produces bad fruit. You can tell what a tree is like by the fruit it produces. . . . Your words show what is in your hearts. Good people bring good things out of their hearts, but evil people bring evil things out of their hearts. I promise you that on the day of judgment, everyone will have to account for every careless word they have spoken.*
>
> Matthew 12:33–36 CEV

If you saw a restaurant with golden arches, you'd assume it was McDonald's, and maybe you'd begin to salivate for fries. If you saw a shoe with a swoosh, you'd guess it was Nike, and maybe you'd have a sudden urge to run. Those are brands—little signals that tell you what you're getting into. Sort of like if you saw apples growing on a tree, you'd realize you were looking at an apple tree.

Jesus says that your words are kind of like that. They're like signals of what's going on inside you. If you go around spouting negativity, or you slam people, or you complain about everything, that's a symptom that not all is well inside you. By the same token, if you speak positively, or if your words are kind and encouraging, that probably means you're allowing God to change you. Or else you're really good at covering things up. And while some people attempt to fake others out with sugarcoated words, the truth comes through eventually.

But there's another reason Jesus warns about words. It's because he knows how powerful they are. He knows that words have the power to heal or to kill. He knows that someday we'll all have to explain what was going on with our words . . . and there might be some apologies due.

Think about it. Have you ever been hurt by someone's words? Is it possible that you've hurt others in that same way? So listen to yourself. Listen to the tone of your voice and the words coming out of your mouth. And think of those words like a brand—a signal of what's inside. If you don't like what you're hearing, ask God to help you change it.

My Prayer

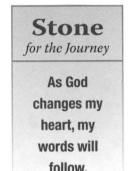

Dear God,
Help me to realize that my words are important—but not as important as the condition of my heart. Please help me to sound and look more like you.
Amen.

Stone
for the Journey

As God changes my heart, my words will follow.

Final Word

> *Remain in me, and I will remain in you.*
> *No branch can bear fruit by itself; it must remain*
> *in the vine. Neither can you bear fruit unless you*
> *remain in me.*
>
> John 15:4 NIV

Melody Carlson is the award-winning author of around two hundred books, many of them for teens, including the Diary of a Teenage Girl series, the TrueColors series, and the Carter House Girls series. She and her husband met years ago while volunteering as Young Life counselors. They continue to serve on the Young Life adult committee in central Oregon today. Visit Melody's website at www.melodycarlson.com.